Building Bridges in Board Dynamics

Be More Confident, Competent and Conscious as a Value-Creating Board Member

Dorrit Kromann

with contributing author Leo Smith

Building Bridges in Board Dynamics
Be More Confident, Competent and Conscious as a Value-Creating Board Member
© 2025 Kromanns

ISBN: 9781068394300 Paperback

Published by: Inspired By Publishing

Building Bridges in Board Dynamics

be More Confident, Competent and Conscious as a Value-
Creating Board Member.

© 202.. Kronana.

ISBN: 9781068394300 Paperback

Published by: Inspired by Publishing

The strategies in this book are presented primarily for enjoyment and
educational purposes. Every effort has been made to trace copyright
holders and obtain their permission for the use of copyright material.

The information and resources provided in this book are based upon
the authors' personal experiences. Any outcome, income statement
or other results, are based on the authors' experience, and there is no
guarantee that your experience will be the same. Indeed, it is understood
that in any business enterprise, and there is no guarantee
that one will have similar results to the author as a result of reading
this book.

The author reserves the right to make changes and assumes no
responsibility or liability whatsoever on behalf of any purchaser or
reader of these materials.

Dedication

To all the board members and aspiring leaders who strive to create meaningful impact, may this book inspire you to build bridges and empower you to be more confident, competent and conscious in your roles. Together, let us foster environments where diverse perspectives thrive and value is created for all stakeholders.

Acknowledgements

I would like to start by sharing my gratitude to the many people who have been part of this project. Thank you for helping me build a bridge between the hard and soft areas of board work.

First, I wish to mention the six members of the board who headed the organization behind the making of this book. You have each fulfilled your role as a professional board member while also being willing to add the "soft areas" into the boardroom, both done to explore what this book is all about: answering the question, "Is it at all possible to apply psychodynamic and psychological thinking into the board landscape?"

Thank you to Annette Lang Skovbølling, Ashley Morris, Lesley Antoun, Paul Diponkar, Peter Koefoed and Phaedria Marie St. Hilaire.

The board is truly a diverse one. I thank you all for your time without payment, and all your fruitful input and participation.

The book is written in cooperation with other authors, as well as with contributions from various places, including seminars I attended and people who have simply listened. I wish to thank Klaus Majgaard for sharing your knowledge on producing books and encouraging me to write the book; several of my board colleagues including Jens Christian Refsgaard, Claus Juhl and also Jacob Aqraou for proofreading just before publishing; and my family Christian, Conrad and Carl for reading, giving input and listening. I thank everybody who has participated a lot and a little; some I can mention, some I need to leave out for confidentiality reasons.

Thank you to Leo Smith, whom I met after watching a presentation by his company. You created the chapter "Talent-Based Board Work" with all your deep knowledge on talents and organizational mentoring. Your positive approach has supported the rest of the book.

While I already had the synopsis for this book in mind, writing it in a way that people can understand and connect with is a whole other ball game. If I hadn't contracted with Chloë Bisson, the CEO of Inspired By, I would never have been able to produce and publish a final product. Thank you, Chloë, for your time, your inspiration and for pushing me.

Whether thanks to coincidence or destiny, sometimes the people you need are right in front of you. This goes for Sabitha Jørgensen who has produced all the drawings for this book, making it more than just words. Thank you for understanding the essence of each chapter and for making simple yet clear illustrations.

Another person who became part of creating this book by coincidence is Deborah Schindelman. You, as the reader, would probably have a much harder time digesting this book if Debbie had not changed the high theoretical language into well-flowing proper English. Moreover, Debbie has brilliantly managed to condense this book into a quick guide. Thank you, Debbie, for the marvelous work altogether.

While creating this book, I also worked on podcasts for additional support. I wish to send a great thanks to you all, from someone who has just done their first take as a new host. Thank you for sharing your knowledge on board dynamics.

The podcasts are published by Progressive Media. A special thanks to Ashley Morris and Dan Wilson who have been patient with me as I learn how to record and edit the podcasts.

The inspiration to develop this book came from the works of Steen Visholm, Birgitte Bonnerup and many more in the field of psychodynamic organizational psychology. Andrea Petrone connected me to many important people while writing this book, including Lesley Antoun and Helga Svensson, proving just how supportive this network has been.

Thank you to all.

Foreword

As the Board of Directors overseeing this book, we commend the authors and emphasize the critical importance of understanding boardroom dynamics.

Dorrit Kromann has expertly led our board with professionalism akin to any business board, guiding this project similarly to a start-up company and with sincerity and innovation. The diverse perspectives within our board have been instrumental in shaping this book, which serves as a guide to navigating board dynamics. Aptly enough, the reflections on the actual dynamics happening in our board have added to the understanding of generic board dynamics.

This book bridges human elements with goal-oriented strategies to enhance efficiency in a turbulent world. It underscores that while diversity is crucial, it alone doesn't ensure performance; active engagement with and mentalizing diverse perspectives is necessary for effective decision-making.

The book provides examples that offer insights into understanding and working with board dynamics, enhancing your ability to apply these concepts to your own board activities.

Dorrit Kromann and contributing author Leo Smith have created a valuable asset for board members seeking to explore psychological dynamics and behavior in the boardroom as well as those focusing on enhancing boards to become high-performing.

Additionally, the accompanying website offers further learning on topics we had to prioritize secondarily, such as "Leadership, Followship, Fellowship", "Cultural Influences in the Boardroom" and "Mentalization in groups." This resource enriches your knowledge of the theories behind the book and furthers your understanding.

Our board members have also shared practical experiences through a podcast series related to this book, facilitated by Dorrit's guidance. Other experienced board members have shared their views as well, which provides even more support for the reader.

By reading this book, you'll be inspired to analyze the business and to apply the understanding of psychological, organizational and cultural dynamics in your own board roles.

We express our gratitude for the creation and organization of this book.

The Board Dynamics' Board of Directors

Contents

Introduction

Do you understand board dynamics and what they do to make a board high-performing and its members value-creating?

Understanding board dynamics is crucial for a board of directors to transition from mediocre to high-performing. Effective board dynamics involve how directors interact, communicate and make decisions collectively. A well-functioning board leverages diverse perspectives, fosters innovation and adapts to change, all of which are essential for organizational transformation. Addressing issues like power imbalances, groupthink and conflict management can enhance board performance. Boards that prioritize inclusive dialogue and strategic decision-making can better navigate challenges, ultimately improving company performance and shareholder returns.

This is why you should take a deeper dive into understanding board dynamics, whether you are new to the board world or are a knowledge keeper with years of experience in board work.

I am a professional in the fields of organizational psychology and neuroaffective psychotherapy. I also have spent many years training in reflection and self-reflection. In my experience, consciously working with these elements can help build a bridge between the task at hand and the dynamics of the board.

By looking into board dynamics, I can better understand the interactions, relationships and behaviors among members of a board of directors – factors that have a direct influence on their effectiveness in decision-making and governance. The dynamic will play out in how members communicate, collaborate and resolve conflicts, affecting the overall performance and strategic direction.

With my focus on understanding the dynamics, I have been able to play my hard skills at the best moment. This, of course, with the knowledge that I had the rights and the responsibility to ask questions and contribute in order to be part of a value-creating board.

My experience with board dynamics goes way back, even before I stepped into it officially.

I had my first board position when I was 18 years old. My goal was to lead our building's co-op in the right direction and make the most out of our money to create a nice place to live. I was young and full of energy, so I jumped right into the job. Today, I am happy that this type of board is now protected by legislation because they often consist of amateurs – and I say that with the greatest respect. Until I got my first instruction on the topic, I knew so little about the overall responsibility. And I knew even less about what trouble you could be in being part of a board where some people feel all their wishes must be granted, some are arrogant and some just wish to live in peace. People join these boards for different reasons, some of which are personal – as opposed to professional – which make the dynamics go wild.

Currently, I am on various professional boards and an investor. I both chair boards and contribute as a regular member. I have also been elected by a large democracy (customers), been appointed by the owner and been chosen specifically by the owners to be elected at the General Assembly.

In this book, I will share my experiences and also stories from other board members. I will apply the knowledge I've gained so that you too can become a confident and conscious member of a high-performing board. My co-writer Leo Smith will also be sharing his lessons.

While working on this book over the last couple of years, I met many board members from around the world and have also spoken to many others about what board dynamics are like worldwide.

The interesting individuals I spoke to confirmed my own international board and investor experience: Boards today are vibrant, under pressure from major changes in the environment and a lack of time, struggling with too many new areas to understand, have more and more material to prepare for and have a requirement to apply good governance with a focus on diversity.

The board has become an organization under pressure. Board members must be conscious of working on the tasks at hand in the most efficient way possible in order to create value for the business. Therefore, board dynamics as a topic is becoming increasingly important to understand.

Throughout the process of writing this book, it has become clear to us as authors that board dynamics is a topic in its infancy and will become an asset to value-creating boards.

Understanding the historical development of boards on a global scale is essential for being conscious of which stage of development you and your particular board are in and what challenges you face today.

Understanding that boards are different because of legislation, on both the regional and national level, and also by culture, business area, type of company and as their own unique entity, is the basis of a conscious ramping up.

This book is for you, the board member, if you wish to step into the next era of board work: to become conscious of your role and how you take on that role; become confident in taking on your responsibilities and duties and; act competent when fulfilling these responsibilities and duties.

To get the most out of reading this book, you need to know your board's responsibilities, good governance practices and your duties and rights as a board member. Look at this book as a complement to what you typically learn in any one of the excellent university or business school board programs around the world or business-specific board education, such as a utility-company board education or high-school board education.

The prerequisite for this book is that you know about board legislation and good governance. In case you are not familiar with the board framework, you may have some knowledge of the underlying theories: psychodynamic organization psychology, learning, person-environment theory and positive psychology, and find it interesting to know how it is applied to board work.

In this chapter, you will be introduced to the world of boards, the historical development and today's challenges. You will understand what to expect from the content of this book and what to learn.

In the end, you will discover how this book has been organized as a company with a board. This book was developed so you can apply your understanding of board dynamics to your own board work. It is a practical presentation, with examples of how the dynamics may play out, including action plans and a couple of exercises to give you some practice in how to explore.

Boards, Historically and Now

The board of directors, as you know it today, has evolved over the centuries. Research conducted by Franklin A. Gevurtz shows that the concept of a governing board began as early as the 12th century.[1] The research is based upon structures in Europe with documentation from Flanders, Italy, England, France and the U.S.

The first boards developed from town councils and merchant councils who convened to make decisions and operate together.

Overall, the development of corporate boards grew as a governance mechanism for merchant societies (such as The Hansa) or merchant cartels (like the Dutch East India Company). Only later did they evolve into a governance mechanism for large business ventures with passive investors.

The historical foundation of boards will provide you with an understanding of how boards work today and why you may find dissonance between the requirements from corporate law and what boards, in reality, have to cover. In other words, going from a place of making common decisions and working as a common operation of individual units to a place with a focus on governance in economic and organizational development in a particular unit.

Historically, the underlying concepts of corporate governance are:

- Shareholders elect the directors (normally, annually);

- A group composed of peers that act together to make decisions, and;

- The board has the ultimate responsibility of selecting and supervising the corporation's senior executives (especially the CEO).

Jumping to the present day (with the past in mind), boards were previously built on old-boys clubs and most were not run professionally. For example, many SMEs are led by family members or friends because, traditionally, a board group is an exclusive and almost secretive "club." Ninety-five percent of recruitment to Danish boards in 2019 took place via networks, but this is rapidly changing. Various surveys show that companies with a professional external board achieve higher turnover and productivity than their competitors.

The workload has grown due to the higher expectations, challenges and more complex needs of shareholders and regulators. This has led to changes in the board structure with more committees such as audit and risk, compensation, technology, strategy etc. Fortunately, the period has also shown a positive change in workload. The period of "death by PowerPoint" has passed; now, more compact material is presented to the board.

With less homogeneous boards comes more dynamics. This is a fertilizer for innovation and learning.

As boards' agendas become more overloaded with items such as legislation, regulations, environmental, social and governance implications, technology and technological security, social media, diversity, sustainability and the reporting on these areas, there comes a need for pre-processing topics prior to the meeting. This is similar to how audit, risk and remuneration committees review these topics prior to the meeting.[5]

This challenging environment and the new role of the board require it to be active, embrace diversity and work together in the same way a team works together in an operational organization.

The professional world has worked with organizational development in the operational organization for many years. With this new active board consisting of many different types of individuals and having global requirements and impact, the board is becoming an organization in and of itself. Therefore, it needs just as much attention to leadership and organizational development as an operational organization.

In board education programs, the chairperson is taught to manage the meeting. For example, students used to be told at the board programs, "The most important role of the chairperson is to make sure that something intelligent is happening at board meetings." However, now it has become: "The most important role of the chairperson is to lead the board and frame the 'semi-temporary' organization which lives at the board meetings throughout the year but also interacts in between." The term "semi-temporary" is used because the board continues being a board in between the meetings, but members do not work together as an organization during that time. The board and the organization interact with each other through the chairperson and the CEO, but also directly through committees with employees and board members. It is a very difficult balance to manage. But committees are evolving, and as the amount of skills and tasks the board has to take on increases, the number of committees will rise. This is yet another call to focus on board management.

The board today can be regarded as an independent organizational entity that has to be handled, supported and run exactly as an operational unit within the organization. That is to say, the chairperson should have leadership skills, team building is a prerequisite for members who are working together on the board, one-on-one meetings are required etc. Most importantly, board dynamics must be managed and be part of the room for the leadership.

Board dynamics is simply the way board members interact with each other. As a result of the new, active, diverse board with constant global change challenging it more than ever, understanding the dynamics has become ever more important.

And why do we care about understanding board dynamics? Simply because if we are not aware of the intangible elements of working in a group of human beings, the board will fail and stop working on the task at hand. After having worked with this book, I hope you have a better understanding of what board dynamics is and its importance.

Mapping Types of Boards

What I see is that, throughout the world, boards of directors are used and structured very differently. On top of this, the legal foundations of a board vary greatly from country to country.

In North America, you will find that good governance has just recently changed. Here, *not* having the CEO as the chairperson of the board of directors is advised. In France, the CEO is still often the chairperson. However, that is starting to change. Meanwhile, such a practice would be a breach of good governance or even be illegal in a limited company in the Nordics. In Germany, the board is a supervisory body and has very strict rules on membership, democracy and transparency.

While there are differences between countries, the purpose and the overall responsibility of a board is the same: To ensure that the business – whether it be private, an NGO, volunteer, publicly noted, government-owned, and the like – is a running business with a CEO, an agreed strategy, has a financial plan and is compliant with legal requirements, all run according to good governance at all times.

The stage the business is in will affect the degree to which the board fulfills this responsibility. This is because a small start-up company runs differently from a private school or a publicly-listed global company.

So geography, business type, stage of the business, experience level on the board, the C-level and many more factors affect the board work of today. But one thing is universal: the board consists of human beings and together, they form a group with a purpose. To understand this effect in a board is to be conscious of board dynamics, ultimately with the goal of being a better value-creating board.

How do you define the characteristic dynamics of the board you are entering? What could you expect from entering the board? The answer is, you don't. Instead, this book will provide you with the tools needed to explore each of the individual boards you are entering.

What you wish to do when characterizing your new board is to look at the following parameters:

- **Board Organization.** The number of members, owner-appointed members, democratically-elected members, elected members at the General Assembly, executive committee, chairperson and vice chair, volunteers and so on.

- **Regulations.** The legal requirements.

- **Finances.** Are they economically liable?

- **Compensation.** What is the minor salary, large salary, warrants and options?

- **Partners.** What are the strategic partnerships in place and who are the stakeholders?

- **Operational Organization.** Who is in top management? What is the organizational structure?

- **Type of Company.** Is it private or public, volunteer, listed, political, run by an owner, subsidiary, a start-up, a scale-up etc?

- **Geography.** That of the customer, the owner and its physical location.

- **Business Area or Industry.** Finance, retail, public, consulting etc.

- **Governance.** What are the requirements on how to run the business in an ethical, transparent and accountable way?

- **Culture.** What are the shared set of values, beliefs and practices that shape this organization?

- **Product.** What kind of product (tangible or intangible) does the business offer?

Note that by gauging these characteristics, you will likely still not get what exactly to expect from the board in question. But by looking into these parameters, you will be better prepared to understand the landscape you are entering.

Book Overview

Above, you have been given a short introduction to the board landscape. We have looked at board evolution, what boards are like today and what the requirements and responsibilities are for the specific board member and the whole board.

What is your role as a board member besides what is described in the law of the country you are in, the shareholders agreement and the rules of procedures? Your role, outside the formal area, is to create value for the board. In this book, you will learn how you, as a board member, can show up as a conscious, confident and competent contributor.

To do so, the following chapters will take you through how to understand dynamics, how to work in committees and finally, how to understand your own talents.

Chapter 1
The Framework: Above and Below
the Surface of a Board

This chapter introduces you to the framework which you may hold in your mind throughout the whole book. The framework will provide you with mental boxes to put your knowledge in as presented in the following chapters.

Chapter 2
Agency and Boundaries: How to Be Confident in the Boardroom

In this chapter, we will go into the two common denominators in every boardroom: agency and boundaries. You will become conscious about what you bring to the table and accountable for how you do so. You will also get to know where to intervene and where not to. You will know the boundaries and be conscious about crossing them and what the effects of doing so will be.

Chapter 3
How the Dynamics Play Out in a Board Above and Below the Surface

In this chapter, we'll look at how the rules and roles of board members are created, whether they're visible or not, and the obstacles that can be created due to feelings and informal roles that have been created.

Above the surface is where your role as a board member is well defined and boundaries are explicit. Below the surface is where elements that are not visible, defined or recognized play out to create soft roles and soft boundaries.

Chapter 4
Personal Emotional Dynamics Worth Understanding

To explore what is happening below the surface further, it is necessary to go deeper into some basic elements of the psychodynamic field. This will help you understand what is driving the dynamics of the unknown and undefined spaces. You will be introduced to these basic elements and how they may play out in the boardroom.

Chapter 5
Core Group Dynamics Worth Understanding

Particular situations play out in the boardroom, affect what is happening below the surface and influence dynamics above the surface. Things will happen and you just won't understand why. In this chapter you find an exploration of core group dynamics such as how biases change our view, what happens in crises and others.

Chapter 6
Talent-Based Board Work

After a deep dive into psychodynamics, we look at talents on the board.

The better you understand yourself, the better you can act, be present authentically and have the agency to fulfill your task.

In this chapter, you will get familiar with the background of different talents in relation to the board task. You will get insight into how to use your talents and understand others' talents in interaction with the rest of the board. The purpose is to help you play out your talents in the right way to fulfill the tasks of the board: to set the strategy, to ensure a running and compliant business and to hire the C-level in the operational organization.

Chapter 7
How to Understand Dynamics in the Board Committees

Looking into the future, the structure of board work will most likely change to include more and more committees. This chapter will explore more deeply this challenge from a dynamics point of view.

In today's boards, the overload of information and tasks are exceeding the limits of board members' capacity to get into the details. Board meetings with 400 to 1,200 pages of material are not unusual. More and more committees are appearing in the board landscape to leverage knowledge before a condensed summary is distributed to all board members for a decision.

It requires a certain level of discipline to make these committees work to the benefit of the board. That is, to not be too closed while also condensing the material. Committees can interfere with the board's connection with the operational organization as some members will meet outside of regular board meetings. Information will inevitably be transferred between the board and the organization.

In this chapter, you will get an introduction to how to show up and fulfill your board role in a committee and how to be conscious of breaching boundaries with the purpose of creating value.

Chapter 8
Quick Guide

A summary of what you have learned throughout the book is found in this chapter. This is your go-to chapter if you just want to know the one-liners. There will also be references to the previous chapters' more detailed presentations.

Conclusion and Onwards

Finally, a bit of perspective and a recap is needed.

How a Board Created This Book

I have structured this book very uniquely. The production of this book was run very much like a business so that I may live my own word. It was made with as much diversity and bridge-building as possible.

I appointed a board of directors to head the book-writing, similar to a start-up business. I am the owner and investor. The board consists of seven members with myself as chair. I also headed the operation (the writing process) and, of course, I carried out the job as an author. This is indeed complicated, having four roles, but it is not unusual to see this dynamic in a start-up; it is set up so very close to a business board. At our board meetings, we even took 30-minute debriefs to explore our own dynamics.

For a full discovery of the organization, please go to the end of this book where you will find the vision, the annual wheel, the board members as per publishing of the book and all the suppliers and assistants.

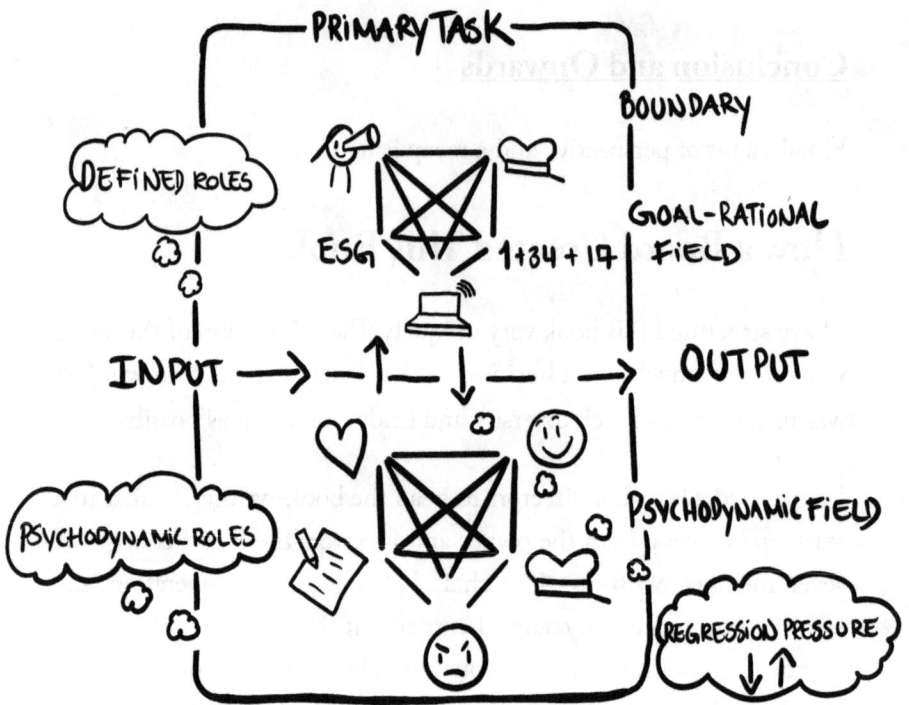

Chapter 1

The Framework: Above and Below the Surface of a Board

In the previous chapter, you were introduced to the history of boards, the board landscape and their effect on board dynamics. The interactions, relationships and behaviors between and among board members influence decision-making. Therefore, it is essential that you are able to navigate the dynamics of this environment.

The title of this chapter includes the words "above and below the surface." But what does that really mean? The illustration explains this with a model that you can use to analyze what happens on the board in the explicitly defined area "above the surface" and what is not seen, understood or acknowledged "below the surface." Moreover, it shows how all the elements could interact. This is a simplified way to explain what psychodynamic systems theory is in the context of how we can use it in board work. Throughout this book, you will get further into how to use this theory in practice in your board work.

Think of the model as an iceberg. The water is the surface of consciousness dividing the known from the unknown. This analogy can help you understand the importance of the mysterious depths of the work on the board.

This model has helped me understand where I stand and how I can fulfill my role in any organizational context I have had to navigate. I have carried this knowledge over to my board work and have noticed how much unseen beliefs, actions, behaviors and feelings influence board work, both with beneficial effects and hindrances.

Therefore, the idea of this book was born from wanting to make board work more efficient through an understanding of the dynamics and by applying the psychodynamic system theory.

In this chapter, I will introduce psychodynamic system theory so you can have your own framework for navigating board dynamics. It can be used as a container to store all the knowledge you gain from this book.

PERSPECTIVE

The Importance of Understanding the Framework

Organizations are living organisms. Since boards are also organizations, they are alive as well. These days, boards are managed and run the same way as operational organizations and have a similar organizational structure with subgroups (i.e. committees). As such, it has become necessary to understand and work on boards the way we do operational organizations, which includes leadership, followership and fellowship.

As board members, we are human beings who enter a room and form a group. We have roles and responsibilities and must tackle a task together. We have rights linked to our roles. For example, the chairperson has the responsibility of leading the group. The chairperson also has the overall responsibility of ensuring that the board oversees the owners' interests and that the objectives are met while still being compliant with regulations. These are tangible tasks.

However, there is a non-tangible aspect as well. Organizations consist of living human beings. In addition to their hard skills, they bring all their personality, feelings and thoughts to the group. These people all have ambitions, dreams, families and traumas that they bring with them to work. We all deal with our joys and struggles in our own ways, influenced by our culture, upbringing and life experiences. And some of these things turn up in disguise at the workplace, just below the surface.

When we apply soft roles to different people in the organization, it shows how much human beings bring their individual personalities to the workplace, both consciously and unconsciously. It plays out in interactions and how people relate to each other. If you think about it, you could probably identify that one person in the organization who is constantly complaining, the one who always remembers everyone's birthday or the introverted one who never wants to go to company parties. This person fulfills the hidden desires of the whole group. So, understanding how soft roles work is useful in helping you identify which role you are filling in the organization and how to avoid the one you do *not* want to play. Being conscious of these dynamics allows you to show up with confidence and competency. And that goes for any type of group you are a part of. Trust me. It makes a world of difference. This is what it means to look at your board through the lens of a psychodynamic organizational systems framework.

For more than 100 years, group dynamics have been researched and implemented in workspaces.[6] But until recently, it has not attracted the attention of boards – with the exception of some boards that practice board evaluations to comply with good governance. The subject was not addressed in the various board education programs I was a part of, neither by the business school nor by sector-specific programs. However, my personal study of the subject has served me well.

An example of how I have been able to use my organizational psychology knowledge is on boards with double roles. For instance, in a board where investors are also members, founders fill the C-level roles or investors assist the founders in creating leads. When I found myself in these situations, I pointed out these double roles – my own and the others' double roles. It may sound simple, but this is the sort of thing we tend to forget when we are fully engaged in our board work. Even though these roles are defined and everybody is aware of them, they activate feelings about who has the right to decide and when.

There may not be a struggle, but you can look at the situation through the lens of this framework to understand when a process gets halted. Ask yourself, "Are we bringing the different roles into play in the wrong group? Am I, as a board member, being operational? Are the C-level executives in the operational organization making decisions in their role as owners?"

As a concrete example, you can run a strategy process for a typical start-up whose founders are also the C-level in the operational organization. First, ask the founders, who are also majority owners, what their dream is. Next, bring it to the board members and get their input and commitment. At this point, it is the board that must ensure that the strategy is implemented by the operational organization. So, why don't you just talk directly to the founders since they are both majority owners (it's their money) and the C-level (they will implement the strategy)? If you have a professional and active board, they are the ones who are responsible overall, both legally and towards all the investors. They are the decision-makers responsible for implementing the founders' overall vision, as decided at a shareholders' meeting. If the founders do not agree with the board, they (as majority owners) can fire the board at a new shareholders' meeting. But they cannot just start changing direction in their daily work without having the approval of the board. This is important because you cannot fulfill your responsibilities without the possibility of making decisions within your role. That is exercising your rights as a board member.

So, by understanding the situation through the lens of the psychodynamic organizational systems framework, you can acknowledge the difficulties of both transferring power to the board and letting go of overall power. In addition, you can recognize the structure, roles and responsibilities of the board. In this way, you make things clear to yourself and the people involved so that you can all comply with the way of working that was agreed to.

Another example I would like to let you in on is how the organization for this very book – set up and run like a professional business – has also shown that being conscious of roles and boundaries is important. I have had meetings and done podcasts with the board members, individually. You could probably acknowledge and accept this as it is an action that supports the vision and the task of this organization. But at the same time, something happens to the dynamics. Let's say I promote one member to another. After the interaction, that particular member would now have another relationship and another history with me, which the other board members do not have or know about. What does that do to the board dynamics? Does the word of that particular member become more important? Does it split the board? Many other questions such as these could be explored, as well. So, after having interacted with individual members, we brought it up at the next board meeting so everyone is aware and informed of what has taken place. In this way, we opened up the floor for exploration and ensured that hidden fantasies or feelings would not disturb the future work of the board.

To conclude, I will quote Bonnerup, "Sometimes, it is the process in the psychodynamic field which makes things work against all odds. And at other times, the best-planned process will stall due to incomprehensible psychological processes."[7] In today's boards, you will benefit from using the knowledge of the psychodynamic field to find what is pushing against and what is pulling toward the end goal.

PITFALLS

Pay Attention When Using the Framework

Have you ever experienced getting stuck in a conflict or not getting any problem-solving done in a group setting? I have had many experiences like this. Both being stuck myself and seeing the group getting stuck while trying to innovate. So, what is at stake and what can go wrong, both when you don't explore the dynamics or when you explore too much?

If you don't view board work through a psychodynamic organizational systemic framework or explore the dynamics at all, you may miss your own underlying contribution to a conflict or the stagnation of the group. Or, you may not see what others bring to the same situation. You could end up debating elements that are actually underlying feelings, thoughts or fantasies playing out rather than the actual items on the agenda. By exploring psychodynamics and understanding the roles and responsibilities, you can see what is really going on.

If you do not understand your roles and responsibilities, you cannot take on your tasks and legal obligations. You could cross over to other roles and end up being liable for areas you do not have influence on. My only advice for this is to voice your concern at the board meeting and get it recorded in the minutes. If nothing changes, resign from the board. Remember that your reputation in the board world is at stake and most importantly of all, you are legally bound.

I was once stuck in a situation where there were differences in the interpretation of the roles of a board and a parallel board. There was a power game going on by keeping the parallel board as a separate board. But the biggest problem was that the overall board was legally responsible – not the parallel board. I had a major struggle navigating this power game. Eventually, the issue was resolved with the legally liable board taking over. So, the responsibility and decision-making were handled by one board, the one who had taken out the insurance.

In a board, you may see that there are different agendas in the minds of different members. It is the responsibility of the chairperson to reconcile these by voicing the differences. Otherwise, it is not possible to progress. Bear in mind that differences like these will always come up. You will very likely go through several power struggles like the one above, especially when new members are elected.

What You Need to Know

There is a need to apply leadership and organizational understanding to board work. You can use this framework to gain the necessary understanding and be conscious during your own board work.

So, What Is an Organization?

The McKinsey study defines an organization as, "a system with a common primary task and possible sub-tasks. The organization has boundaries with respect to the rest of the world (surroundings). These boundaries may be physical or marked in other ways."[8]

So, a board is an organization with a common task. A physical boardroom or a virtual meeting room is where the board meets and defines its tangible boundaries.

Primary Task

The primary task is the mission that the organization has set out to do together. It is the reason for the creation of the organization and the purpose of its existence. In business terms, we talk about mission and purpose, or simply, why this organization is alive and what it does.

It is essential for the organization to be acutely aware of the primary task. If you cannot define a reason for its existence and its purpose, then you do not have an organization. Instead, you have a collection of people who happen to be in the same place at the same time.

Input and Output

By understanding the board as a system, you can look at what is entering and what is exiting the board. These are tangible. The inputs are the hard skills, the material provided and also the people forming the group. The output is what the group brings to the outside world. For instance, decisions for the operational organization to implement or for the owners to know about. Likewise, we as human beings bring our material into the group and take material out of the group.

Boundaries

Boundaries in an organization make the distinction between being in or out of the group. In order for these boundaries to work properly, they must be clear to all – both inside and outside. You can also find boundaries within the board, formal as well as informal.

Roles

A role is what defines how you participate in a particular group. Your formal role is what you have been explicitly asked to do. It is how you support the organization by working on the primary task in order to achieve the overall goal. It is usually well-defined. Your informal role is the one that you take on or are pushed to take on through interactions between members of the board. You may do this consciously or unconsciously. These roles may also serve to hold unbearable feelings for other individuals in the group and the whole group.

Goal-Rational Field

The board may be viewed as having two faces: above and below the surface. That is, the goal-rational field above the surface and the psychodynamic field below the surface.

The goal-rational field is the conscious area in which all the identified tasks, roles, boundaries etc are visible on a board. This area is described in legal and governing documents, such as policies, terms and references, bylaws, rules of procedures, insurance etc.[9]

In the goal-rational field, the board members know which goal they are working towards and who has which responsibilities, meaning, what contribution is expected from each member.

The Psychodynamic Field

The psychodynamic field is in the subconscious realm. It is the unconscious zone where relations play out. For example, you can see both individual relational patterns derived from childhood and group-relational patterns developed as a culture in a particular group. In this field, you can also see the preconscious processes which are unknown to the individual. Think of this as similar to when you've entirely forgotten an old school friend's name until the very moment you see their face again and it simply pops back in your head.

Equally, there are unconscious processes, repressed thoughts that are difficult to access. In this field, emotions such as jealousy, rivalry, sorrow and happiness are present. This is also where enthusiasm and desire to work together live, as well as the blossoming of talent in relation to the other members of the board and people in the organization.

Regressive Pressure

With the goal-rational field and the psychodynamic field, you may notice that a conflict in one puts pressure on the other. For example, suppose the board is working on a financial crisis that cannot be easily solved. In that case, the group may end up blaming and putting personal pressure on the board member who supports the business area which is mostly financially affected. From the psychodynamic angle, there could be a personal conflict between two board members which may impact the goal-rational field, manifesting as an inability of the board members to make a decision.

Since starting my professional life, I have studied and worked in the field of organizational psychology because it has always been relevant to all of the businesses I have operated in. I gained some of my knowledge from personal experience, and some from my business school programs. But the one framework I have most benefited from is the model on psychodynamic system theory developed by Visholm.[10]

I still remember in 2003 when I first saw how this model could be used to help me navigate the professional space by understanding the dynamics taking place in organizations. It was a full-day session at Roskilde University in Denmark. That day, we were given a structure and a timeframe to put words to the thoughts, feelings and fantasies materializing in the temporary organization we had built together at the university. That evening, I came home to my family with a big smile saying, "Finally, I found someone who speaks the same language as me! Finally, I have a framework to structure my thoughts, feelings and understandings about organizations." That did not mean I had found nirvana. It simply meant that all the conflicts, misunderstandings and strange behaviors I had previously observed were at last free to be explored.

Since that day, I have benefited from using this framework to track what is not apparent to the eye. As I grew from being in the operational business to being a board professional and investor, I saw and continue to see a lack of attention to board dynamics and how that influences the decision-making process on the board. Today, efficient organizations must also include an understanding of how boards work.

By understanding and keeping in mind the above system and elements, you too can use this framework as a skeleton for the rest of the input you will be introduced to in the following chapters.

What You Need to Do

Here, you will find a to-do list that will help you better understand the framework.

It is best to have a particular board group you would like to join, or you can reflect on one you were once a part of. Guide your thoughts and understanding of this board using the following five steps. In case you do not come up with any insights, you may want to seek information from other board members and discuss.

Five Steps Towards Understanding the Framework

1. Understand the goal-rational field and how it influences the dynamics

   Ask yourself the following questions: What is the business and the primary task of this particular board, according to the formal documents? (This could be strategy, legal requirements, owners etc). Which official and visual boundaries are present in the organization? Which roles and procedures are formally described for the board? (For example, the chairperson, committee, annual wheel etc).

2. Understand the psychodynamic field: what's going on below the surface?

What tasks does the board take on, besides the official ones? For instance, do any of the board members work in the operational organization as consultants? Which unconscious or invisible boundaries do you notice and why do you regard them as boundaries? Think about the boundaries between elected members and appointed members or diversity groups, and the like. Which soft roles are given to the board members or others participating in board meetings? For example, who is constantly pointing at the clock to move on, who is always critical etc?

3. Make a draft of the board using the systemic psychodynamic model

List down the following elements: Primary tasks, boundaries, roles, leadership, input and output, resources, and regressive pressures (conflicts).

4. Attend the First Board Meeting

Take on your role as a board member. Observe what is happening in the group above and below the surface and within yourself.

5. Explore Your View of the Organization

After attending the first board meeting, explore your view of the organization from the point of view of the systemic psychodynamic model.

By going through these five steps, you can get an idea of what you will encounter with this board and further explore your views based on the first meeting. These reflections are not a one-time activity because the board is a living organization and people change. Repeat this task whenever major changes happen or at least once a year.

My Dream for New Board Members: Learning by Doing

I truly believe that the best possible way to enter and understand a board is through learning by doing. This is exactly the foundation of this book and yields the best results by far. If, in any way, you can get access to the chairperson of a board you would like to join, ask to start as an observer. In case you cannot get an observer position, you could alternatively ask for an onboarding with the chairperson and the CEO, ask for material on the board's work and for information on the business you are entering.

How to Recover

We have so far discussed why organizational concepts are essential for understanding and working on boards, and how the framework can be used. You have also been shown examples of what could go wrong. Below is a short guide on how to come back as a board member if openly addressing organizational dynamics doesn't work out.

Maybe you are on a board that is not keen on the idea of self-reflection. In this case, you should decide on your own if this prevents you from working efficiently and being confident and competent on the board. If not, find your own personal process such as grounding yourself so that you can prepare for the non-verbal communication that happens when a below-the-surface power struggle happens and feelings come out. Or, you may work behind the scenes. This does not mean you are undermining the board. This only means you are addressing invisible interactions not during the meetings themselves but, for example, during a coffee break. Additionally, you may support the people who are not being heard by repeating what they say. This way, you demonstrate that showing trust influences others to show trust. Sometimes, if the chairperson is open to it, you may also bring up your observations with the chairperson directly.

When you focus on the dynamics, you may lose sight of other elements such as the primary task. So, always be curious when you are met with something that you don't feel is justified or doesn't feel right in your gut. Note it down and pay attention to see if it continues. Accept that there is not always time to work below the surface. Apologize if you bring it up at an inconvenient time and ask when it could be added to the agenda.

Finally, you may also find a trustworthy co-board member to bounce your ideas off of when you need to test out your own biases and analyses.

In general, you will always need to balance your input on board dynamics. What I have learned is that if you are attentive during emergencies, are genuine in your desire to get the job done and notice the group dynamics when they happen, you will rarely be wrong in bringing up the subject of dynamics at the right time. And if you are, an apology is always a good way to get back on track.

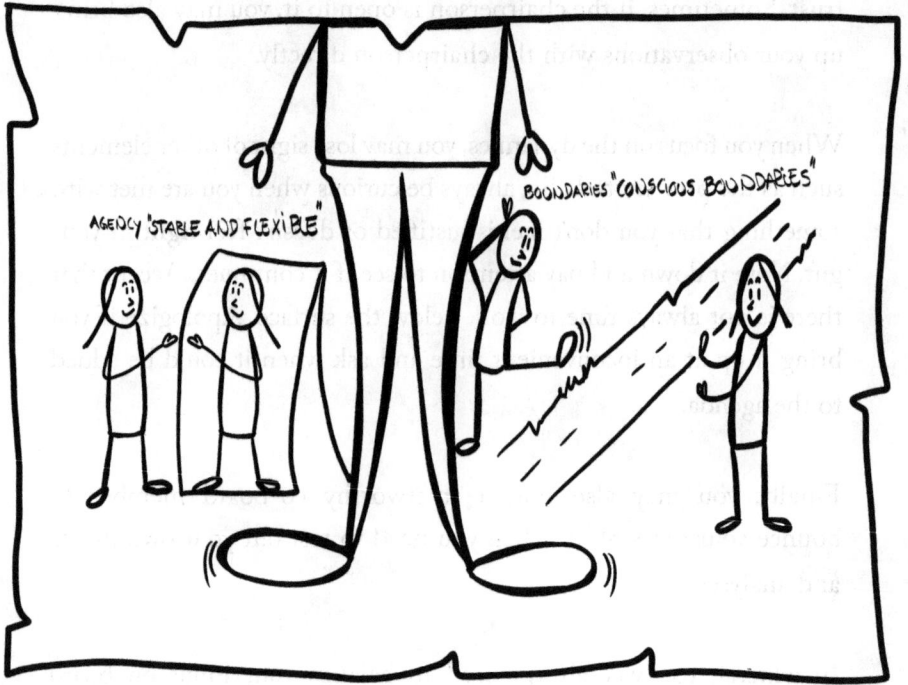

Chapter 2

Agency and Boundaries:
How to Be Confident in the Boardroom

After looking at the board landscape and being introduced to the framework, you are now ready to dig deeper into how to apply this new way of working to your own board work.

Are you new to boards? Or are you maybe already experienced in board work? Are you a current board member or chairperson looking for more board positions? Or perhaps you are looking for a new board position?

If any of the above questions apply, then you are probably well on your way. You have most likely already gotten a board education, looked into which businesses you would like to add value to, posted it on LinkedIn, started networking and even applied for an open position.

It takes courage to put yourself out there for a new board position! No doubt when you start on-boarding, you will be extremely eager to take on the responsibilities and rights as a new member in a successful manner.

So what do you need to do? Well, it is actually pretty simple: Show up with agency and an understanding of the boundaries at play so you can leverage your hard skills and soft skills at the right time. As opposed to boundaries, which most of us can relate to as a barrier, agency is possibly not a word you are familiar with. Agency is, in short, the feeling that you have the power and freedom to act independently, make decisions and influence outcomes.

Despite my organizational knowledge, I was not prepared for my first board position. I would have benefited from understanding agency and boundaries. I needed to know how they help a board member be confident and competent at a board meeting, with the ultimate goal of adding value to the organization and honoring my responsibilities as a board member.

Throughout the last decade, I have learned the hard way how important it is to show up with agency and understand the boundaries. I have crossed boundaries and, by being conscious about having crossed them, it became an asset. I was able to make an exit plan and return to my role on the board.

I have also gotten the feeling that the surroundings were "running me" rather than me stepping up to fulfill my responsibility and exercising my rights to do so. When you show up with agency, you are accountable for your own actions. Or to put it another way, you are in the driver's seat of your own "personal behavior" vehicle, free to navigate in the environment as is and according to your consciousness of the boundaries.

In this chapter, we will get deeper into agency and boundaries. We will look at how a board member can show up with agency and how to understand boundaries. This will give you the foundation needed to become more efficient as a board member. In other words, you will learn how to use your awareness of agency and boundaries to make you more confident and competent as a board member.

The Importance of Understanding Agency and Boundaries

The board is the highest authority in the organization and so, the organization relies on the board to set direction. The board sets the strategy and oversees the company to ensure it remains a successful business both now and in the future. They hire C-level roles to run the business. If you do not show up with confidence and competency on the board and in the board's committees, you may not get your voice heard nor understand what you, as part of the board, have decided. This means you would not be exercising your rights nor taking on your responsibilities. That being said, you would still be just as responsible as any other board member should anything go wrong.

You were most probably elected to the board because you have hard skills which the company requires. For example, marketing, social media, technology, environmental, social and governance, go-to-market strategy, industry, change management, human resources, finance, legal, top-level management etc. You may also be on the board because you were elected by an owner, which is often the case when the company has obtained new capital from angel investors, existing investors, Venture Capital companies etc. Finally, you may be on the board because you were elected by representatives, such as employee-elected members, customer-elected members or other groups who have the right to democratically elect members.

When you are on the board, you would like to do a proper job and take advantage of both your hard and soft skills. A prerequisite for this is you feeling confident enough to take on the responsibility.

Confidence, in this context, is the ability to believe in your own abilities and judgment; to accept and trust yourself.

Competence, in this context, is the ability to perform tasks successfully, using your hard and soft skills.

If you know your own strengths and weaknesses, you can set realistic expectations and goals. You can relate to, communicate with and give and receive feedback in a respectful manner towards other people and yourself. With confidence, you may also have a better foundation to explore and understand your own boundaries, the organization's boundaries and when you cross them.

With this kind of confidence, you have the basis for playing out both your technical expertise and your interpersonal skills. That is, applying your competence at the right time in order to create value for the organization.

The theoretical background for this handbook is psychoanalysis, psychodynamic psychology, learning and positive psychology. In all these areas, two common denominators stand out when exploring board dynamics: agency and boundaries. These parallels are what we, the authors, see as part of the foundation for showing up confidently and competently in the boardroom. You may look at it as two pillars of your board work.

Agency, generally speaking, can be described as the capacity or ability of an individual or organization to act in a given environment. In other words, you are conscious of your own actions and feelings and you are accountable for them. As a person, you can show agency in your interactions with others and through the application of your intellectual competencies. In relating to others, you can show agency in a group by acting with accountability. For instance, if a board member disagrees with a majority decision, the board member may say with agency, "I do not agree with this decision but I respect the defeat and the majority. I will of course work to ensure the best possible implementation." If the board member does not act with agency, they may cut off communication, undermine implementation, or create conflict in the board.

Agency in a group is highly important when making vital decisions like one would in a board. Black-and-white hat roles are a way to ensure agency in a group by appointing specific roles to specific members, ensuring various views.

Boundaries are, essentially, limits that define what is in or out of a system. They may be individual or apply to any kind of organization. Boundaries are there to protect the individual or the group. It is important to explore them, especially when crossing them.

In an organization where people show up with agency, people are less likely to act with underlying and often unconscious agendas and will probably not try to blame others for their faults. It may sound like an impossible utopia, and that is what it is – impossible. Be aware that you won't always feel like you have a sense of agency or are in complete connection with yourself. But, the more you know about your own values, the better you can act in accordance with your authentic self.

Likewise, the better you see and understand both explicitly defined and unspoken boundaries, the better you can fulfill your role and ensure that you do not take on a responsibility belonging to someone else. For example, if you notice that the chairperson does not take charge of running the board meeting, you may feel compelled to take over. But this would be crossing a boundary and would undermine the role of the chairperson. Or you may find yourself in a situation where you or another board member may be required to take over, such as in the case where the chairperson needs to leave the meeting due to an emergency. In the latter case, the chairperson should hand over the responsibility.

So, being conscious of your accountability and being acutely aware of declared and invisible boundaries when you enter a boardroom is part of the foundation of your confidence and competence.

PITFALLS

Pay Attention When Analyzing Agency and Boundaries

Without agency and being mindful of boundaries, the board and the committees may "malfunction." That is to say, there could be things such as confusion and a lack of trust. Needless to say, these things can impede the progress of the work of the board.

You may experience confusion and uncertainty when boundaries are crossed unconsciously and when members do not fulfill their roles. This is exactly what occurred when a chairperson was deeply involved in the daily operations of the organization. Their double role as both majority owner and CEO caused the board to start acting as an advisory team not able to assume accountability. The board had the legal responsibility, but the chairperson was deciding on their own when and for what they wished to involve the rest. Because of this, the board members were liable for things they were not aware of and had no influence over. The board had to take up legal and compliance risks that they had no knowledge of and had not addressed or handled beforehand.

When you do not apply agency and are not conscious of the boundaries, you could experience a confusing group dynamic. Some members will dominate decision-making, and there may be blocking behaviors in the group or a general lack of direction. This is where your chair should take control of the board meeting and, in the example above, take action and go towards the majority owner to redirect the roles and responsibilities according to the law and rules of procedures.

The confusing dynamics in such a situation may turn into an environment with a lack of accountability, conflicts and miscommunication. For both board members and employees, there is a risk of stress and burnout. There is also a risk that the board members may choose to resign.

Case in point: One member chose to resign from her position during a major crisis in a private boarding school. Based on information available to the public, it could be said that she had resigned due to a malfunctioning board, a problem that is likely to show up during a crisis. You may find yourself in a similar situation. In cases where you are not heard, you will need to evaluate your own position as a board member and ask yourself if you cannot fulfill your duties, live up to your responsibilities and exercise your rights. If you cannot, it would be necessary to take action by either requesting the chair to react or to resign.

To give another example, let us talk about one committee where trust was not established. Their meetings had no real purpose since no charter was given to them by the board. The operational organization thought it was supervising the committee's work and the board members were interested in the strategy of the committee's topic so that they could fulfill their responsibility. However, nothing was produced and no more meetings were planned.

Upon further investigation, it turned out that the group had no agency. This was caused by anxiety. Their actual goal was perfectionism, which led to defensiveness when questions were asked. So from there, the base for exploration was gone. There was a fear of the board members' authority and, as you could guess, fear when crossing the boundaries between the board and the operational organization. Uncertainty and the lack of structure could have caused the committee to become rigid, with members taking sides instead of standing on common ground. In such an uncertain environment, the lack of agency became visible. Committee members were not accountable, instead defending themselves and avoiding showing their lack of knowledge. So, no exploration was done and the committee never reconvened.

Finally, agency by structure could apply to budgets, PowerPoints etc. You may end up in a situation where the structure controls the outcome to the extent that no new input is allowed and you end up in a "death by PowerPoint" situation. The solution? Leave room for debate. Structure your agenda so that you let board members know when the item on the agenda needs input, or is up for a decision or for a debate.

What You Need to Know

Agency

To many, agency is a difficult term to understand and even more difficult to apply to oneself and a group. You may be able to relate to agency as it was described by one of the CEOs I work with: "I know agency because I always show up accountable for the decisions I make and [for] my actions." The definition above is one way to be present with one kind of agency. From the psychological point of view, we talk about individual capacity. "Here, we mean the capacity to experience and use complex patterns of thinking, behavior, emotions, physiology and interpersonal interactions. Here, agency represents an internal state and not a behavior, although agency often initiates and shapes behaviors."[11]

In the Neuro Affective Relational Model (NARM) therapeutic model by Laurence Heller, there is a difference between states and behaviors, where state is the current emotional and physiological condition and behavior is actions to the state or environment. The following scenario illustrates this difference. Let's say, at a board meeting, you feel taken advantage of by another member because they are using your words to support their statements by quoting something you said while on a break. You may be hoping that the other members recognize this and do something to remedy it.

At the next meeting, you decide to talk to the board member in question rather than simply wait. The action of speaking to the other board member is not what is referred to as agency. In this example, speaking up is the *behavior*. *Agency* is about your relationship with yourself in which you recognize and honor your needs and feelings. In the above situation, agency means acknowledging that you are feeling taken advantage of and deciding that this is not working for you anymore.

Agency drives behaviors. Honoring one's own needs and feelings presents the possibility of acting, or not acting, in support of those needs. Agency sometimes gets mistaken for empowerment. While they are related concepts, agency is more the capacity to act, not the action itself. Empowerment is about relating to external experiences and other people, whereas agency is about relating to internal experiences and oneself.

When people are able to connect to how they organize their inner experience in the face of external challenges, including painful realities such as domestic violence, discrimination and other forms of oppression, they gain an increased capacity for agency in their lives.

Here is an example of how agency works in a committee treating the subject of cyber security. The committee on cyber security consists of security personnel from the operational organization and board members with either an interest in the topic or expertise in the technology. The major task is to be NIS2 compliant, which is the EU requirement. To comply with NIS2, the operational organization analyzes and implements the requirements according to the regulations. The board is the party responsible for compliance and needs to know what is being accomplished. In the committee, the operational organization and the board members meet regularly to discuss what is being done and which questions are pertinent, from the board's perspective. To develop ideas, verify compliance and fulfill the NIS2 requirements, the committee must have a confident and safe environment in which to work together. This means being conscious of the boundaries, roles and responsibilities. That is, the committee is the group that prepares material for the board and the full board is the group that makes decisions together. In this particular committee, there is mutual respect and trust that everybody is working on the same task. The members show genuine interest in the work underway and take responsibility for their own input, thereby creating an environment where insecurity can be acknowledged and addressed. As such, the committee is well prepared for board meetings with cyber security on the agenda.

In groups, and in general, agency is not the freedom to do whatever you want or to make choices without restraints. Restraints may come from the history of the group, such as when you enter a boardroom as a new member. At the first meeting, you try to understand the group's practices based on the history of the board or the committee. For example, I remember my first top management meeting from my time as a new manager. I was early and found a place to sit. I felt really nervous and awkward. But it was not until the next meeting that I understood why: I had chosen the seat where the CEO usually sits. History played out in real life and I certainly did not feel agency at that meeting. Today, I know that I felt uncertain, but did not feel that the space was open for this uncertainty. I was wrongly engaged with the environment.

As a board member, the key takeaway is that you must be conscious of how various kinds of agencies – whether personal, group or material – are used in the boardroom while paying attention to how these encourage and discourage interactions.

Boundaries

We have acknowledged the importance of agency, individually, in the group and structurally. So, the second part is to be aware of the environment you are working in. Unlike agency, most people can relate to boundaries. It is a common word, defined as a line or limit that marks the edges of an area, distinguishing it from other areas.[12] We know about boundaries from the football field (when the football is in or out of bounds) or from property (showing which piece of land belongs to which owner).

Boundaries, in an organizational context, are defined the same way. But what is important to remember is that, on the board and in any other organization, some boundaries are not visible. Crossing them has an impact on the dynamics in the boardroom.

You should view boundaries as complex, permeable membranes. They are zones where interaction, negotiation and mutual understanding can occur rather than just viewing them as strict, impenetrable dividing lines.

In psychodynamic organizational theory, understanding the boundaries of an organization makes the difference between being in or out of the group. To work properly, these boundaries must be clear to everyone – both from the inside and the outside.[13]

A board is limited in that the members are not operational. Meaning, they do not carry out tasks in the operational organization. If you are on the board of a start-up, for example, you could cross this boundary because you are often in a situation where the founders say, "All hands on deck!" In a case like this, the most important thing is that you are well aware that you are crossing a boundary.

This awareness is important because one of the primary tasks of the board is to ensure that the organization is compliant with external requirements and internal policies. So, if you are a part of the solution, you may be biased based on your insight, knowledge, pride, stubbornness etc. If you don't know where the organization begins or ends, you can lose your orientation, just like being in space without any gravity or visible walls to anchor you. You will stumble and feel lost because things are not as they seem.

On a board with elected members, you may see them group together and sometimes even put up a boundary between them and the other members. For example, in an official election process for a public-private utility company, six members of the board are elected politicians from each of the three municipalities. At the beginning of the election period, it is announced that these members are consulting their own experts from their respective municipalities. This is an announced and visible crossing of the boundary between the board and outside the board. As such, all board members are aware of this crossing.

On the other end of the spectrum, a system that is too rigid, with boundaries that are too strict, will die. For example, in one board, presentations from the operational organization were not to be discussed or revised. It was as if the operational organization was running the board. The decisions were already made before the board meeting had even started and no input or attempts at discussion were taken into account. This situation was discussed during the "board's own time" and the procedure was changed. However, when changing procedures, the board risks falling back into old patterns. Change often feels like a threat. That perceived threat may cause conflicts both above and below the surface, making falling back onto previous practices seem easier.

The formal system (above the surface) is shown in the organizational chart of the company or entity and includes the board, the owners or investors etc. In the informal system, you find groupings that exist due to personal connections, membership to the same political party, professional arena or shared opinions. You may also find groupings by gender, race, age, religion, geographical origin etc. The latter are areas where, in today's boards, we work under the label of diversity. Before diversity became a topic on the agenda, boards tended to be much more homogeneous. Non-verbal communication and tacit understanding were part of the meeting. Just like when you meet up with good friends – you know what they mean; no need to explain.

On today's boards, you still have this unspoken understanding. But now, there are new kids on the block with different shapes and colors, so communication needs to be more direct and clearly expressed. Otherwise, diversity can never become an asset to the board, and even more importantly, to the organization. As a new board member, you may speak up if you experience something that excludes other opinions, people or groups. This could be done either as a subject on the agenda or a statement, such as: "From my position, I may be unfamiliar with the way of working on our board. However, I find we did not give time to listen to Jane when she voices her concern about the lack of women in management."

Other ways to express your concern is to bring it up during the "board's own time" or to raise the point with the chairperson after the meeting by calling them privately.

Both informal and formal systems are important for achieving the primary task of the board. The primary task is the main objective that any organization must achieve to fulfill its purpose. Informal systems can greatly contribute to achieving this. Just like when you disagree with someone you know personally, most of the time, it is just a matter of finding a compromise or making a decision that is mutually respected. However, when it is someone you do not know, you are more likely to distance yourself and not reconcile. For instance, when discussing with the delivery person who tossed your fragile package to the ground instead of putting it down safely, you may not be able to find common ground. On a board, you may discover that you listen more openly to the board members with whom you relate best. On the flip side, you may not be critical enough of their statements because you are biased.

To illustrate this, let's look at a private school founded on Catholic values. The purpose of the school is to form and educate the children based on explicit values written in the formal documents. The Catholic board members seemed to be the caretakers of these values. Their statements were taken as input to ensure that the values of the school were not undermined and were not questioned.

On another board, a profile analysis was made and the talents in the board were analyzed. It turned out that the group was high on optimism and innovation, which left little space for criticism. Therefore, the board created a "perform critical view" topic in the plan for board meetings. This formal system ensured that the importance of making a critical evaluation was recognized. In this way, they set a structure and made a boundary where everybody was aligned with this critical phase.

As a member of the board, you can voice what you see when appropriate, but it is the chairperson who leads the board and the meetings. The chairperson maintains the boundaries of the board by doing three main things.

First, they look inward from the chair position. They do the board work on the primary task, which is to ensure a running and compliant business with a well-functioning operational organization for the benefit of the owners. Second, they look outward from their chair position. That is, they look at the work of the CEO, the committees and the informal sub-groups and what happens around them. Plus, they pay attention to what happens in the surroundings.

Last, the chairperson should survey the boundaries – who is part of the board and who is not. They should take note of how input, production and output balance out across the board. This way, the chair will not need too much information from the operational organization but have enough to lead it. They must also keep watch if the boundaries are crossed and understand why.

You, the board member, have the formal right to be within the board but at the same time, you may feel as if your voice is not equally heard.

Many boards today have a variety of members appointed by the owners, members appointed according to their skills matching the company and members elected by the employees. On one board there was the same number of members from each group. Each member had equal rights and responsibilities, and with the equality in numbers in each group, you would expect that it was a balanced board. But in reality, the owners were always in a position to overrule because they, in the end, could dismiss the board. The professional board members with high seniority spoke with more authority. This left the employees with uncertainty and often less influence.

Systems are marked by boundaries. A board is a group that works as a semi-temporary organization starting with the welcome statement and ending with the final task of the "board's own time." They do not actively interact with each other outside of board meetings. And, of course, there is the time allocated to socializing before and after the meeting.

When you traverse a boundary in a system, it is marked both physically and mentally – such as the physical boardroom where the door is closed as the meeting commences, and the mental role each of the members and participants takes on when the meeting gets underway. You can joke and tell stories about vacations before the meeting, where everyone has the same voice. But during the meeting, you are quiet and show followership towards the chairperson who is running the meeting. You may observe how participants change when entering the meeting, clarifying both formal and informal roles. Or you may notice how a board member dresses differently at a board meeting and at their daily job.

Whatever you may observe as being open boundaries, tightly closed boundaries, sub-groupings or exclusion, you should ask yourself what the board or board member, in particular, is defending itself or themselves from. Could it be from too much information, a crisis on the management level, personal difficulties, lack of knowledge etc? It is here that you get your footing and begin to understand the space you are working in.

Many boards have a structure with meetings four to six times a year. There may be special committees that support the board, such as in publicly noted companies that are, by law, required to have a remuneration and an audit or risk committee. Other companies also have this committee structure so that they can "chew" the material with the operational organization before entering the full board meeting.

The members of the committees include both board members and employees from the operational organization. Therefore, by being a member of such a committee, you would be crossing boundaries and must be aware of it. How does this situation create innovation and how does it create inertia? Note that the boundary between the operational organization and the board has been blurred in this particular committee.

Boundaries are important to board work and good governance makes it clear that board members cannot play an operational role. If it is necessary, you must be aware when you are crossing the boundaries and know how to go back.

Boundaries are necessary, but they could also hinder your work at hand. To be competent, you need to know the boundaries because the skills you bring to the table should be applied at the right time and towards the right subject, with agency. Boundaries form a structure. As a conscious structure, they make the board a safe place. Transferring knowledge is done at all times in the boardroom and with the use of structural elements such as the agenda, PowerPoint etc. Likewise, your awareness of your talents is a structural element in addition to being an element to open yourself up.

You may, as an individual, explore the boundaries and express the boundaries either at the meeting or directly with the chairperson when boundaries prevent innovation and decision-making. The same goes for crossing boundaries.

Your consciousness about boundaries, whether personal, group, organizational or structural, is the way to create an innovative and safe board.

What You Need to Do

In this section, you will find two exercises on how to practice agency and boundaries. They focus on you and yourself, instead of the organization. If you do not practice your own agency and set your own boundaries, it will not be easy to work with these elements in an organization. While defined boundaries are easy to understand, it may be difficult to accept the boundaries and understand the consequences of breaching them.

In the bonus material that comes with this book, you will find many more exercises on how to practice agency and boundaries in the organization. It is not straightforward and not everything may work for you, so pick and choose what suits you.

Your Own Agency

As soon as you have felt your own agency once, you will continue to recognize exactly when you show up with agency. You will not always be able to be in this state, but it may be a good idea to spend some time exploring with yourself, a friend, a peer or a coach.

If you would like to examine on your own, you need to reflect upon your understanding. This is best done by writing down your feelings, putting the paper aside, and then going back the next day to discover your own story.

If you have a friend, peer or coach, you may want to bounce ideas off this person and get some feedback on where you show up with agency.

This may be done as follows.

Reflect about an area of board life where you are feeling frustrated, stuck, hopeless or ashamed. For example, you do not feel heard at the board meetings.

From an agency perspective, identify elements of the story that do not match the feelings that the story reflects. Explore by being curious as to why these areas do not support the frustration, stagnation, hopelessness and shame that you feel. For example, during a debate, one board member may have reflected on your input or another board member may have repeated it.

Think about how it feels to examine these areas that do not support the feeling of frustration, stagnation, hopelessness or shame. For example, ask yourself how it is that you were not heard.[14]

<u>Your Own Boundaries</u>

To work with your own boundaries, try the six following steps:

1. Get a clear view of your emotional, mental, physical and spiritual limits by naming them; ideally, you write them down. What do you accept? What makes you feel uncomfortable?

2. Tune into your feelings by becoming aware of the need to set or maintain boundaries. The feelings – often anger – will show when your boundaries are approached. Communicate your boundaries, especially if they are breached often.

3. Give yourself permission to set and hold your boundaries.

4. Seek support if you think it is troublesome to set and keep your boundaries. This could be from a friend, peer or coach.

5. Be assertive by communicating clearly and respectfully when your boundaries are crossed. Be specific on the crossing and your expectations for future behavior.

6. If you are not used to setting and maintaining your own boundaries, start practicing by setting boundaries that are not threatening. For example, if you do not feel that you are heard at the board meeting, you may start by preparing a specific input with two texts in advance for a particular item on the agenda. If you are not heard, you may raise your hand again and present the second preparation. Speak loud enough and with precision.[15]

How to Practice Working in a Conscious Way

Throughout the book, you will be given various ways to explore the psychodynamic elements, talents and related situations. By becoming self-aware and aware of dynamics in the organization, you will benefit from being able to ground yourself.

Two specific exercises I have used, and which could help you as well, to become present and aware are the following:

Exercise on Being Present at a Board Meeting (or Wherever You Are)

At each point in the board meeting agenda, be sure to sit up straight in your chair, feel your feet on the ground, sense your inner state, look around the room at each person and regularly close your eyes for a second and note your sense of the board as it is at that very moment. Every now and then, remind yourself what your role is, what you currently feel, and what your thoughts and fantasies are.

Exercise to Verify Your Thoughts, Feelings and Fantasies

Note down on a piece of paper what your thoughts, feelings and fantasies are on a specific subject. Put the paper aside for a day and return to see if you are still thinking, feeling and fantasizing the same way as the day before. If yes, why? If not, what has changed and why?

How to Recover

In the section above, you were introduced to examples of what can go wrong when you do not show with agency or are conscious of the boundaries. We also looked at missteps when making the effort to develop agency and create awareness of boundaries.

In this section, you will get a list of possible actions you could take if the results are not forthcoming, if you feel a lack of agency and do not know why or if you keep running into and crossing invisible boundaries.

Explore your own sense of agency on your own time by asking yourself if you can feel another agenda driving your behavior, if you feel an urge to gain control and power or if you feel the structure of board work is holding you back.

Show up with your own agency by being conscious and accountable for your inner state and actions. By showing up with agency, you will most likely influence agency in the room and create an environment for innovative and respectful board work.

Look at the primary task on the surface. If board work leans towards forgetting the primary task and starts focusing only on the psychodynamic field, remember that your first priority as a board member is to be accountable for the primary task.

When focusing on the psychodynamic field in an inexplicit and reflective way you may find a way back to the primary task. The problem is when the board is caught in a basic assumption state, which you will learn about in later chapters.

If you would like to encourage the development of an environment with agency, try showing trust toward others. You can cultivate this by asking for help instead of offering help or solutions. This is because, by doing so, you show that you trust that the people around the table actually have something to offer. In addition, you are daring to show vulnerability.

If crossing a boundary initiates a malfunction in the board or the committee, voice what you see is not working.

If you cross a boundary and take on tasks and roles in the operating organization, point out the crossing and prepare an exit plan from the organization so that you can return to your role as board member. An exit plan includes: time, task, handover, communication to relevant stakeholders, preventive actions and measurement of when to step back.

You may find various other ways to explore your own agency and identify your boundaries. Finding what works for you is a personal journey. In general, you know when you show up with agency if you have tried it once. It is an internal sense and the result is gaining respect from others towards your appearance and behavior. Likewise, working consciously with boundaries also shows respect. As one committee member who understood boundaries very clearly stated, "Remember, it is the board who decides and we, in this group, do the preliminary debate."

Chapter 3

How the Dynamics Play Out in a Board Above and Below the Surface

You have now been introduced to the psychodynamic organizational systems theory framework, which is the idea behind this book. It sets up the structure for the rest of what you will learn here. However, in our context, this theory is only valuable and relevant if you can use it in your board work.

In this chapter, you will gain insight into how board dynamics can be understood through the lens of this framework and, as such, go from having unconscious to conscious knowledge about psychodynamics. With this new understanding, you and the board can then acknowledge and address it. However, always keep in mind that the elements in this book can never represent the whole truth. Everyone has their inner view of who they are and what happens. As such, they have their own interpretation. For example, you may be convinced that you need to please others to be welcome or that you need to be the smartest in the boardroom to be worthy of membership. This, along with your expertise, forms your individual convictions, beliefs and views about the given situation. This is why we benefit from sharing each other's views to seek a better understanding of the whole.

To understand the dynamics of boards today, it is necessary to understand interactions in both the goal-rational field (above the surface) and the psychodynamic field (below the surface). By observing an organization, you may look above the surface where rules and roles are defined and discover that the defined rules have a strong impact on the dynamics.

For example, one person wears multiple hats and therefore needs to switch between roles and responsibilities. In addition, you will also learn to look at what may be happening below the surface in the psychodynamic field, where unspoken rules and roles play out.

In the unconscious organization, psychodynamics may create obstacles or, in the best-case scenario, support a value-creating board. Of course, the whole point of this exercise is to become conscious of the dynamics so that you can catch where board members, or the board as a whole, get stuck.

Below the surface, our feelings and informal roles are engaged. These may be transferred to the goal-rational field where we are task-oriented. But there are also dynamics that can be transferred in the opposite direction, to the psychodynamic field.

In the following examples and explanations, the framework will be developed so you can better understand how to use it to grasp the dynamics on the board as well as relate it to your own thoughts and experiences.

The Importance of Understanding Dynamics

How do I get myself heard and understood? This is the most important question you must ask yourself as a board member – not to become a superstar or be highly visible, but because it is necessary to get your message across to assume your role and fulfill your responsibilities. You need to be conscious of when to draw attention to yourself and when not to.

My experience has been that it takes some time before you find your place on the board and manage to fill your role. If you have roles that you usually take on below the surface, you should be aware of it when entering a new board position. Let me illustrate this with a personal anecdote. In my career as a board member, one of my priorities has always been risk management. This means I am in charge of ensuring that the operational organization always presents the risks of each of the board's decisions. At one meeting, I had been extraordinarily attentive and I sensed, through indirect comments from other members, that the presentation of risks was taking up too much time. They would say things like, "Well it does not say it directly, but in this other document, it is mentioned vaguely. You cannot expect more…" This made some of the members laugh. They did not think focusing on risks in this particular case was worthwhile.

Despite experiencing this resistance, I continued to address it because it is important to know the liability behind a decision. If I do not have full knowledge, I will not take on the responsibility. So, after a few meetings, I earned the role of being the one who asks questions about risk. Then, after having seen the problems other companies faced when they did not address the risks, I got a bit more credit from fellow board members, both in the goal-rational field and in the psychodynamic field.

Unconscious roles are part of the dynamics playing out below the surface. The act of labeling someone could express itself in roles related to gender, race, religion, cultural origin etc. For example, when I had my first board position at 18 years old as chairperson for a co-op building association (i.e., shared ownership of the building), I was young and therefore earned the label, "the young woman." That was 40 years ago and sometimes I still get that label. I make jokes and this may put me in the young girl's role. To me, we should also have fun on the board. I have become aware of playing this role in the psychodynamic field and when it obstructs having my voice heard as a professional board member.

The visible, above-the-surface interactions are related to the structure of the organization. However, you may notice that the requirements, roles and governance styles vary from country to country. Questions that fall squarely into the goal-rational field may be: Is it a listed company with particular legal restrictions? Or is it an NGO with volunteers or a public/private collaboration with non-profit goals? How are the local requirements and governance regulations met? However, there can be some invisible subtleties that bleed into the psychodynamic sphere. For instance, in the Nordics, the chairperson role is highly respected. In North America, the board setup is evolving towards a double role where the CEO of the company is also the chairperson of the board. In Germany, the CEO role is very powerful in board relations. These are examples of intangible structures that create specific dynamics on the board.

Even the development of this book illustrates how dynamics unfold. Work on this book has been organized as a company: There is a founder and investor, a diverse board of directors composed of nine people, a CEO and three writers. The dynamics resemble that of a start-up company – characterized by lots of uncertainty and no income. I am the founder and investor, the chairperson, the CEO and one of the three writers. As such, I have four roles. I have experienced how difficult it is to keep these roles separate. For instance, I am – between board meetings – in contact with some of the members, but not others. One of the board members is a vendor and another is an expert on psychodynamic theory. For my part, I have the difficult job of managing the finances and overall target, while also being part of the writing team.

The kind of confusion this creates is not easy to handle. We have seen how the lack of clarity sets the stage for conflicts. The solution we used is to consciously identify and recognize the dynamics. We have defined the vision, the roles and the responsibilities in the goal-rational field. We have acknowledged the conflicts of interest playing out in the psychodynamic field. The overall purpose is to write a book in which board members can find concrete tools to become conscious, confident and competent in their board work. This common goal has been our guiding star.

On the board for this book, our meetings were buttressed by designated moments before and after the meeting proper. We start with five minutes of pre-briefing on our own when we arrive. This is our time to prepare ourselves and acknowledge what we have brought from outside of the board. After our meetings, we take half an hour to debrief by sharing thoughts, feelings and ideas that came up when we were together.

This structure created a space for us to look into what may show up for us in the psychodynamic and goal-rational fields.

An experienced board member and business owner once asked at one of this book's board meetings, "From my perspective, time is often a problem at board meetings. So how is the topic of psychodynamics covered using only a short time at each meeting?"

The answer is not straightforward. It is known to all boards that time is a limited resource. This is becoming more and more of a problem since boards are increasingly active and have new tasks to address in a rapidly changing world, such as ESG (i.e. environmental, social, and governance), cybersecurity, governance and reporting. The focus is definitely on the goal-rational field.

The solution is to set aside time at the board meeting for psychodynamics and to require more time from members for extra board meetings throughout the year. As a new board member, you should consider and decide upon your role and resources. Ask yourself: How many organizations can I cover responsibly so that I can provide value to them? Why do I want to be on the board? What is my goal? Does it comply with the goal of the board and the organization?

After having asked yourself these questions, you can start to understand the invisible dynamics by looking at the board with the above elements in mind. Take a moment with each item of the board agenda to extract and analyze the situation: What is actually happening right now?

The need to understand the elements of the goal-rational field so that you can fulfill the board's obligations is straightforward. In addition, you may need to look into the dynamics that are dependent on culture, type of company, size of the board, regulations etc. For many people, the new zone to explore is the psychodynamic field where unconscious roles and boundaries influence interactions.

In the next section, we will embark on a third exploration where you will see how regression pressure materializes between the goal-rational and the psychodynamic fields.

PITFALLS

Pay Attention When Analyzing the Dynamics

In the previous chapters and above, we touched upon what happens when dynamics express themselves. To see what can go wrong, you need to examine the interactions to bring awareness to what is not yet apparent to you on the board.

Here, we will look at what happens if the focus on the psychodynamic field redirects the board from working on the primary task.

So what can go wrong if you use your organizational psychology lens too much and too often? Well, exploring takes time and the board does not have enough time, as it is. So starting to voice these elements at a board meeting may be considered a waste of time. You may be seen as unprofessional.

Take a look at a parallel example from a Danish study in 2022 by the DJØF union.[16] This research showed that some employees are tired of special phrases such as "aligned", "I feel...", "curious", "I think..." and "voice", which may indicate that some operational organizations have spent too much time on the emotional area, that the implementation has not been sincere or simply that some people do not approve of the emotional area.

If the board does not have a designated space for exploring, such as "the board's own time" or the chairperson does not consider these elements relevant for the board to fulfill their objectives, you are probably not going to get very far very fast. In this case, you must stick to benefiting from your own consciousness and, as such, use it to show up with confidence and competency.

What You Need to Know

So what should you do to understand the dynamics of the board? You have already been given a brief description in previous chapters. In this one, you will discover more details on how to explore the business of the board which you are planning to join. Here we will apply your knowledge about board work from your professional experience or your board education so that you can better understand the dynamics.

First, we introduce the essentials of the board as an organization. Then, we look at how to explore the dynamics in the goal-rational field. This may sound straightforward, but we need to remind ourselves to be more diligent (as done in the proper due diligence task). You should think about all appointments for a board as an investment. You are investing your time and reputation; what could be more valuable?

Afterwards, we take a deep dive below the surface to explore the interactions in the psychodynamic field. Finally, we look at regression pressure in between these two areas.

There is a dynamic that exists within a person and within any group of human beings. So when you enter a board room, you cross the threshold into this complex play of forces, carrying with you your own inner ecosystem.[17]

For example, before one board meeting, I had a terrible experience with some of my neighbors. They held me responsible for how the contractors building our house had blocked the road. I apologized for any inconvenience but added that the workers simply had to transport their machinery onto the construction site. This made the neighbors even angrier. I was trying to please them and had done so since the beginning of the project by providing information. On this particular day, communication with the contractor had failed. The dynamics in my inner self were to please the neighbors to avoid conflicts and the dynamic towards the outer world was to defend myself against what I saw as bad behavior and being unreasonable towards a single misstep.

At the board meeting, I brought this inner state with me and it showed up as my being defensive in debates until I figured out what was happening within me.

When you look at a living organization, you can apply exactly the same concept as Freud's structural understanding of the inner self. When you add a systemic understanding on top of that, you arrive at a systemic psychodynamic understanding of an organization.

Today, boards are vibrant and work in a diverse environment. As such, it requires a greater focus on what is happening in the unconscious realm. Dynamics above and below the surface make boards get stuck and also make them thrive.[18]

In an organization, you can explore the inner dynamics of the people interacting, like in the above example where my inner state was expecting to be attacked. For example, the chairperson has to ensure that all items on the agenda receive the attention they require. And so when the chairperson asks a board member to keep it short, they may interpret the message as an attack.

The board is an independent organization working as part of a larger organization (the company). By adopting the psychodynamic view of a board, you get a deeper understanding of the board's processes. By doing so, you can be part of the solution, reaping the benefits for yourself, the board and the whole organization.

What Is a Board and How Is It Different From an Operational Organization?

Before joining a board, you need to get an understanding of what a board is, as opposed to the operational organization you are accustomed to working in. This is because you need to act differently. You go from being operational to setting the framework for the company and being in financial control. You are part of an organization that is within the organization and which has overall responsibility and accountability. You have your money, time and reputation at stake. When you understand these premises of board work, it allows you to act accordingly and navigate the board landscape with certainty and proficiency.

As mentioned in the introduction, a board is not a universal unit since it is defined by many external and internal parameters. Consider the parameters listed in Chapter 1 to better understand the business you are going into.

After having understood the business you are in, you must spend some time looking at how the board differs from the operational organization in its overall goal. This is because you may be coming from an operational position or you have most likely held an operational post for many years before entering a board. There are three important differences that you should pay particular attention to: the double goal, the strategy setting and supervision role and finally, being a semi-temporary organization.

The board's top goals are to assume the overall responsibility of setting the strategy, ensuring that the business is running (compliance and finance) and hiring executive management (the C-level).

However, board members do not do anything operational. If you do, you need to make a conscious decision and an intentional exit.

In general, boards follow these simple definitions and rules:

- The board is a semi-temporary organization that exists during meetings typically held around four to six times a year.

- The board has partial information on, knowledge of and interaction with the organization.

- The board does not, in general, interact between meetings.

- The C-suite and the chair interact in between board meetings to prepare for the next one.

- The committees consist of both board members and employees who meet in between the meetings.

The primary task of a board is divided into two parts: to secure ROE (Return on Equity) for the shareholders and to ensure a running business. These distinct goals could open the door to prioritizing stakeholder interests over the organization's survival as an independent entity.

In an operational organization, the management does not have two opposite goals. The management's goal is to fulfill the vision of the company and the departments all have sub-goals to support this vision.

On the contrary, the relationship between the board and the management is different from the one between the management and the departments because the board always looks after the owners' interests. For instance, a listed company may receive an offer from a private equity fund to buy the company by delisting it from the stock exchange (Leverage Buy Out). Depending on the offering price, the strategy and why the company wants to be listed, this may go against the strategy and the company's mission and vision. In this case, the board cannot fulfill its double goal and must choose to serve the owners, which in this case, are the shareholders.

It may be frustrating to be caught between having to create value for the organization, and at the same time, decide on the owners' interest – which can often go against the former. As in the case above, the offered price could be attractive for the investors. But for the organization, it may not seem like it would add value to daily operations. All the strategy work, new products and costs connected with the merger may be counter-intuitive to the employees. You may see a conflict of interest between these two parts of the primary task. It could be a clash between your role on the board and personal values, or other roles you may have outside the board or in external networks.

Fulfilling the primary task of a board is done by setting the strategy, ensuring a running, compliant and financially viable business and hiring the C-suite management. As such, the board is not operational. Practically speaking, it means that you "sit on your hands," ask questions and make overall decisions.

Setting the strategy for the organization and controlling the finances may be two opposing forces. Strategy work is creative and based on innovation and trust. When the strategy is being implemented by the organization, it is the role of the board to oversee that it is done. In addition, it is the role of the board to make sure that the company is compliant with regulations and is financially healthy. So, the board also needs to manage the money. However, overseeing and controlling the budget does not support trust. Balancing this paradox is part of the nature of the board.[19]

Whereas a board is a semi-temporary organization that meets a few times a year, an operational organization meets every day and its members have only one primary organization, of which they are employees.

The fact that the board is a semi-temporary organization emphasizes the need to renegotiate roles, values and positions from scratch at each meeting. In the psychodynamic field, each member brings in new hidden feelings, thoughts and fantasies every time.

No board or organization corresponds perfectly to the psychodynamic organizational description of an open system as is shown in Chapter 1. But by making the discrepancies and paradoxes apparent to everyone, you will hopefully have a better idea of how to act accordingly in this imperfect world. With this awareness, the board is more likely to operate on the primary task without being stalled by invisible and unconscious feelings, personal goals, preferences or fantasies.[20]

Primary Task

As previously described, the primary task is what the organization has set out to do together. The primary task of a board is split into two tasks, which, as seen in the previous example, may sometimes contradict each other.

Legislation and good governance dictate the board's primary task as the general responsibility applicable to all boards. In the following example, you can see how that primary task could be challenged by not actually working on it or by defining another primary task.

In many start-ups, the board exists just to comply with legal requirements or simply to have prominent names backing the company. You may also see a family-run business in which the founder or owner would like to comply with the guidelines of good governance and therefore creates a board, but never really gives up the old one-person-decision structure. Many owners would say, "Does it matter if I don't ask the board? In the end, I have the majority of shares, so I end up deciding anyhow." It is true that when it comes to making a hard decision, the owner may end up being the one who decides what to do. But this is done through a formal process in which the board makes proper notes of the conflict and may even decide to step down. In a case like this, the shareholders are informed of the conflict at the shareholders meeting and a new board is elected. This procedure makes sure that the conflicting interests are out in the open. Without this process, the company may lose the shareholders' trust.

As with any other task, the primary task may be split into sub-tasks. On a board, you may see various roles defined for the board and formal committees. For instance, according to governance for a listed company in Denmark, you should have a Remuneration Committee, an Audit & Risk Committee and a Nomination Committee. On some boards, members with specific competencies may carry out specific sub-tasks in between meetings, such as Cyber Security or Audit & Risk.

Everybody in the organization must stay on task, as agreed upon. This goes for both the primary task and sub-tasks. All this requires coordination and management by the chairperson. It may not be rocket science, but getting off track is one of the reasons many organizations and groups grind to a halt. Otherwise, board work could just carry on without anyone taking the time to look up and verify the purpose and the task at hand.

I once did a revival process with a company in which I started by asking, "Why are you actually doing this? Why are you putting your money at risk?" It turned out that, for many years, the company had been going along developing great products, but did not have the time to check in on the purpose and the primary task. Once that was done, it gave direction and channeled energy into the whole company. It gave them motivation to develop the strategy and find the right product to solve the specific customer need.

In psychodynamic theory, we view the primary task in three different ways: normative, existential and phenomenal. The normative task is the task as described formally. The existential task is the way you as a person or group perceive what the purpose is. Finally, the phenomenal task is what you actually do as a person or as a group to fulfill the task.

This could be worth spending some more time on because, in the boardroom, you may think you are contributing to the primary task but, in fact, something else is actually at stake. By viewing the primary task from different angles, you may discover why you feel like nothing is moving, why you are not heard and why you don't understand the other members' input. To do an analysis from these three points of view, further material can be found on www.kromanns.com/boarddynamics.

So, why might a board get distracted from its primary task? One possibility could be that the board is fleeing from the normative task (which is stated in the formal documents of the organization) because it is too difficult or scary. Or maybe the power system is at stake, so members are trying to hold on to it by escaping from the task at hand. An example could be the transformation from a privately owned company to a listed company. This situation takes power away from the owner and puts it into a democratic election system where the General Assembly and the shareholders make the decisions at the annual meeting. Another reason a board may be pulled away from their task is a crisis. When things go wrong, people tend to go into survival mode, both as human beings and as groups. This could manifest as fight or flight on the board, waiting for the chairperson to do something or two members taking over the conversation, leaving the rest of the board in silence. So how should you react in a crisis situation? You, as a regular board member, cannot and probably should not do much to intervene. This is the responsibility of the chairperson. You can, however, share your observations about what you see and feel.

The role of the chairperson is to keep everyone on task. The chairperson leads the board meetings and the company, not only according to their own ideology and personality but more importantly, to comply with what is required to run the board and fulfill the primary task of the board and the organization.

The chairperson must, at all times, balance the need for hardcore action and process with the need for inclusion, respect and exploration. If one must give way to the other, the pole that was temporarily abandoned must be revisited later, when time allows. For instance, when the topics of the board meeting are financial statements and the auditor's review, you are not going to spend time talking about whether the process could have been done more respectfully by sending out easier-to-read material. But you should absolutely bring it up if the material is sent out too late for the board to have enough time to process the financial statements. Being personally responsible as a board member, you cannot sign the yearly account statement in a case like this. All you can do is submit the financial statement with comments.[21]

The Double Organization: The Conscious and the Unconscious System

In the model, an organization operates in two domains: The goal-rational field and the psychodynamic field. The model is a mental one.

It is an analytic tool used to understand the dynamics and to inspire work optimization in the group.

In the *goal-rational field*, everyone works consciously on the *primary task*. Collaboration between board members and the relevant employees from the operational organization is focused on finding the most optimal solution for the whole organization. The chairperson leads the meeting and delegates work to board members and employees. Members get their authority from the chairperson and by being elected. But authority also resides within each board member, as a person. You enjoy the importance of qualities like your expertise, your willingness to speak up, your sharp thinking skills in the here and now etc. There is a natural hierarchy related to the importance of the sub-tasks of the board. The financial sub-tasks are the most important part of any board meeting. Strategy and compliance are the most important subjects to address at least once a year and upon major external events. A crisis could become first on the agenda at any meeting and may be a reason to call an extraordinary meeting.

The goal-rational field requires that you conform to the rules and the decisions that have been made – even if you do not agree. If you need to discuss further to better understand the decision, you can schedule a separate meeting with the chairperson. In some cases, you could even return to co-members on a subject that you did not fully grasp. For instance, on my board with a water utility company, the government regulations were particularly complicated. I was fortunate that a hydrologist, a professor specializing in water, was on the board. My being able to talk to him after the meeting allowed me to get deeper insights.

The goal-rational field is important for making sure that the board progresses. It is thanks to this field that we know exactly what to work on. We have an agenda and material before the meeting and the strategy of the organization, plus good governance. But each member also needs to have their own sense of meaning from working on the board. If members don't feel that the work of the board has a purpose, or they do not know the objective of their role, then the organization may enter into a non-working position (referred to as a basic assumption group) where people go into the crisis mode described above.[22]

On the other hand, in the psychodynamic field, you are on the playground of relationships. This means relations have no limitations when we talk about understanding an organization through the model. That goes for both when you like the dynamics, as well as when you are overwhelmed by them. If you pay attention to this field during the board meeting, you may find common psychodynamic relational patterns, both on the individual and group levels. You could also see different processes, such as pre-conscious (not yet conscious but easy to access and still having an influence, like being tired) and unconscious (not accessible but still having an influence, like shame due to unreleased childhood trauma).

Boards today are just now entering the area of working as an organization, with a focus on all aspects similar to what is addressed in an operational business. Some boards have designated the "board's own time" where you can discuss how the meeting went and any concerns that may have popped up. But it is not common to bring up thoughts, feelings and fantasies as a talking point when reflecting on what is happening on the board and in the operational organization.

I attended a three-day seminar when I was working on my Masters in Organizational Psychology from 2003 to 2005. During these days, we participated in working conferences using the Tavistock methodology. It was a space for us to explore the psychodynamic field while we were, at the same time, in it. One of these sessions was a real mess, with many conflicts and difficulties with working on the subject of the conference. A long way into the conference, during one of the reflection sessions for all 75 people, we students learned from management that the staff group had had major conflicts. After this was dealt with and became a conscious fact to everyone, we were all able to start working on the primary task again. The problem simply dissolved because we were conscious of it. We got to see in real time how a conflict in one group affects the whole organization in a parallel process. It also underlined how extremely important it is for the board to understand that any splitting, division or hidden agendas can trickle down like a water leak, whether it is a flood or a small drip.

In the psychodynamic field, you find behaviors that seem incomprehensible – things going on and feelings that are disguised as if it were Halloween. There could be rivalry, jealous critiques, zeal or enthusiasm, grudges etc. Let's look at the following example from a board with seven members working during the COVID crisis to keep a business running. There were different opinions on how to keep safe and, at the same time, to make sure they did not go out of business. Everyone agreed on safety first, but everyone also wanted to be heard at all times on operational matters. Of course, this was not possible, since new instructions from the government were often communicated at the last minute. As with most of the world, there was a real fear within the board of dying. This is the kind of fear that pushes us into unconscious acts. One of the members was so eager to get in control because he had a hidden agenda to undermine the chairperson and the CEO. From this crisis, the seed was planted to split the group, stemming from anxiety as common ground. And due to the worldwide upheaval, there was no time, expertise nor competence on the board to explore the psychodynamics of the situation.

The psychodynamic field can also reveal the joy and engagement of working together. As a group, you make it happen, you see the solution bloom and you are part of something that matters. Since the board is a semi-temporary organization that lives during the meetings, it is a joy to gather together and to greet everyone again. You get to reconnect and catch up on the private side, as well. You experience the joy of making the decisions, which you then see bear fruit in the operational organization. You always find joy when you see the rise in the stock price as well as when the strategy materializes.

In psychodynamics, the rules can be bent. Disagreement shows itself in subtle ways through behaviors like teeth grinding, a tough remark after the meeting or eagerness to win the next word battle. This is highly dependent on the relationships between the members, how they reconnected as well as the subjects on the agenda. Likewise, it is sad to say goodbye each time at the end. In psychology, you would talk about the sorrow of departing. You may find this evident when someone quickly leaves to avoid the feeling of sorrow, or someone stays to avoid the feeling of separation and spends time to do a proper closure.

The psychodynamic field is inconvenient, creative and unpredictable. It is difficult to control and manage. As such, the processes in this field are the ones that either make things happen against all odds or make a simple project become a tangled mess. Everything under the surface is as baffling as it is unconscious.

How can you use your own feelings as data points to tell you what is at stake in the invisible zone? After all, your observations are "polluted" with your own biases, opinions, actions etc. However, you may be able to look at your own reactions and interpret them. The following internal dialogue illustrates this process: "I feel sad, I'm down, my mood is low. Maybe I am holding onto a habit from the past (such as being operational)." Another example of internal dialogue might be, "I feel irritation, anger and rage. Maybe my personal boundaries have been crossed (for example, if someone made a joke at my expense)." Yet another could be, "I feel guilt, regret or shame. Maybe I have said something or made a decision against my own values (like, I wish that decisions were always accompanied by a discussion about the impact on the climate – but I was overruled on this matter)." This is how emotional intelligence serves you: by using feelings as a starting point for exploring what is going on below the surface.[23]

Regression Pressure Between the Two Fields

If the organization is uncertain about its task, boundaries and the passage between boundaries, it creates a regression pressure in both the goal-rational and the psychodynamic fields. By regression pressure, I mean acting less maturely than you are capable of as an adult board member. Both are related and you cannot understand an organization if you are not conscious of the processes in both fields.

As an example from one board, the CEO was diagnosed with terminal cancer, leaving the board members profoundly affected. This serious situation impacted both the goal-rational field and the psychodynamic field. The CEO was a founding member and had built the company himself, making him a fatherly figure you could always trust and who knew all about the business.

Looking at the case, I see the regression pressure from the psychodynamic field. The situation triggered the members' fears of their deaths and anxiety, which pushed into the goal-rational field. They had to decide how to ensure the succession and the survival of the company. It was a difficult discussion at that board meeting. The CEO wished to continue working until he was physically unable to continue. But in the end, the chairperson had to let the CEO go so that they could onboard the successor and save the company.[24]

What You Need to Do

In this section, you can find practical advice on what to do. No explanations. No sweet talk. Just actions. That being said, all explanations and variations are described in the previous chapters so you can understand the nuances and the background of these concrete recommendations.

The Goal-Rational Field

You must first familiarize yourself with this field – the primary task, the boundaries and the roles on the new board – before joining. You can do your preparation by searching for the following materials and asking to meet with certain people.

First, familiarize yourself with the website of the particular organization and which board you are going to work for, from A to Z. Do an internet search of the industry, lobby organizations, the organization, the CEO and the rest of the C-level. Also, look them up on professional social networks like LinkedIn.

Ask the chairperson for the strategy, the financial statement and auditors' report, the latest Q statement (financial report), last year's minutes of board meetings, the annual wheel, the organizational chart, the remuneration process, the shareholders' agreement, the Articles of Association, the rules of procedures, the board evaluation, the compliance report and insurance papers. Ask for a meeting with the chairperson and one board member so that you can get subjective input on what the board's goals are and what it is like to work on the board. Find out what the board's three most urgent matters are.

After, analyze your findings by using the following tips.

- Do a pre-due diligence by using the information collected.

- Look at the roles, as defined by the official documents, both legal and internal.

- Look at the organizational structure: the board structure with committees, the chair and the vice chair. Also, study the formal meetings between the chair and the C-level group.

- Write down your take on the primary task of the board you are entering – the normative task. Explore your thoughts about what you think the board's primary task lacks.

- Write your impressions about the boundaries of the board you are joining. Think about what is missing or too rigid on the board.

- Note what you think about the roles on your new board. Ask yourself what gaps you see or if there are too many roles. Are there vacant places? Why?

Getting Below the Surface

Next, you should focus on understanding the psychodynamic field with reference to tasks, boundaries and roles. Find a quiet place and sit down with all your notes and drawings about the goal-rational field. Use your thoughts, feelings and fantasies as your guide in the following analysis. Look into the relationships that are outside the boardroom and other intangible data points.

Identify the relationships. Analyze the relationship between the board and the operational organization: What works, what does not work and what could be different? Evaluate the relationship between the board and the owners or investors. Again, ask yourself what works, what does not work and what could be different. Consider the relationships between the board members. Once again, ponder what works, what does not work and what could be different.

Write down your thoughts, feelings and fantasies on what you see in relation to the primary task. What could be a secondary role of the board? From the analysis, do you get the feeling that the board serves another purpose other than just being a board at the service of the owners?

Write your thoughts, feelings and fantasies on the psychodynamic boundaries of the board you are about to join. Who talks to whom? Who has which relationships? Is there a hierarchy or influence from an authority role or other outside the boardroom? Note your thoughts, feelings and fantasies on the psychodynamic roles on your new board. Explore your own ideas about what you think is lacking.

Make a first draft of the organization according to the systemic psychodynamic model:

- Ask for an onboarding program.

- Write up your own analysis of the board and highlight where you feel competent and confident, as well as where you do not.

- Ask to participate in a board meeting before accepting the appointment to understand how much is pre-agreed, what happens in smaller groups before the board meetings etc.

Take On the First Board Meeting

- Head into your first board meeting armed with the following tips:

- If you do not understand something, ask for more explanation once. If it is still not clear, ask for further information after the meeting.

- If you do not agree with a decision, voice your opinion. But nevertheless, accept the decision.

- Remember to balance being curious and responsible with being conscious of time.

- At the meeting, look at the primary task from a different view. Use the bonus material if you wish to dig deeper into normative, existential and phenomenal. Do you find a parallel shifted task from normative to existential and phenomena, and is it preventing you from working on the primary task? If yes, voice it and let the chairperson lead the board through it.

- Throughout the meeting, look for non-verbal communication and groupings.

- Assess the diversity, inclusion and sub-groupings on the board.

- In case any of the sub-groupings or the communication hinders you or others from expressing opinions, bring it up in a curious and respectful manner.

To close this process, you should establish your own view of the organization following the systemic psychodynamic model after the meeting. Do this by taking five minutes in a quiet place to debrief yourself. Jot down your overall experience, both in the goal-rational field and in the psychodynamic field. The next day, make additions and changes to your notes based on data points from both fields: both hard facts and thoughts, feelings and fantasies.

By working through these steps, you can create your own understanding of both the goal-rational field and the psychodynamic field for your particular board. This knowledge gives you an understanding of the landscape you are navigating. It can make your input and work more efficient and hopefully, you will feel self-assured and capable when entering the room and working with the board. If you are looking into applying for a board member position, work through the steps being fully aware that your input on the psychodynamic field is based on fantasies, thoughts and feelings about the expected dynamics since you have not yet interacted with the other board members. As such, these are your own convictions. But you could use your whole analysis to decide whether or not you are interested in entering the board.

Remember, when you are looking for your first board position, you may be eager to ignore any elements from your analysis that you do not like. But by doing so, you glorify the position and you may find yourself on a board that is different from what you expected and to which you do not enjoy contributing. I say this from experience. I have had positions where I was flattered and encouraged to sign up, so my analytical view was fogged. I had made a bad decision. And so I worked to exit those types of boards without too much turbulence.

Bear in mind that your analysis never ends. You should always be exploring the goal-rational and psychodynamic fields. The board is an organization that is semi-temporary, beginning and ending with each board meeting. Every time you meet, it's almost like an organization starting from scratch. And you too likely come in with a mindset that has changed since the last encounter.

How to Practice

To prepare yourself for a new board position, you can practice before the actual post opens up.

- Define your own board profile.

- Enroll in a board education program.

- Choose three businesses that you feel suited to. First,

go through all the tasks in the task list in Chapter 1, Section 5: What To Do. Test your analysis with other people who are in this line of business.

- Look through your network and find people to contact. Make two groups: One group of people who can support your development and one group of people you would like to contact for a potential board position.

Practice your psychodynamic understanding in your existing organizations by exploring, as shown above.

RECOVERY
How to Recover

In all work interacting with human beings, there will be pitfalls. But don't mull over it too much. Overcoming difficulties is really about accepting yourself when taking on a new job and a new role in an unknown environment. This is uncharted territory for you.

As long as you are well prepared, you can ground yourself and show up with confidence and competency, all the while listening to and exploring what is going on. On the next page is a quick discussion of possible problems and solutions.

Too Much Psychodynamics and Too Little Time

Redirect to the primary task and understand the hindrances to fulfilling responsibilities. When you overthink and overanalyze everything that is happening, it takes time away from the goal-rational field. You may not have time to bounce ideas around since the board is under a time constraint. In addition, if the board is not mature enough to discuss the dynamics, you may encounter so much resistance that you cannot address these types of issues at all.

In such a board, you may work in four steps. Start with addressing what you experience on the "board's own time." If the board does not have the time, then redirect yourself to the primary task and focus on the goal-rational field until there is time. If the board never has time for a debate on board interactions, you may ask for a one-on-one with the chairperson. Finally, if nothing changes so that the board can address important dynamics, you could consider how necessary this is to the board and the fulfillment of your responsibility. You may even consider your membership on the board.

Fleeing Work on the Primary Task

Talk about what you see or talk to the chair. Working as a board and solving a task together could lead to both joy and anxiety, both of which could cause the board to avoid working on the primary task. In this case, look into whether the board lacks competence, and if the work on the board is very sensitive or feels dangerous on various levels. Likewise, ask yourself if people are competing or if the forecast shows major issues. If you recognize any of these or other causes as to why the board is not addressing the task at hand, you may voice it or ask for a private meeting with the chairperson.[25]

Shadow Work

Go back to your board position or address the issue to the chair. If your assignment on the board grows beyond the board and committee meetings, you may be doing shadow work. This work is invisible and also a potentially disturbing dynamic on the board. If you find yourself addressing the operational organization with issues you encounter outside the formal structure, consider whether you are crossing the boundary to the operational organization or whether issues in the operational organization need to be addressed with the chairperson or at the board meeting.[26]

Changes Not Materializing

Make a new decision or enforce the change with support and communication. Imagine that the board decides on a new strategy but the decisions do not materialize either in the operational organization or in the board. You may ask yourself why the changes are stuck in the old way of working. Could it be because the decisions do not make sense when the plan materializes during the implementation or is it due to a lack of resources and competencies? If it is not possible to implement the plan, this critical issue should be immediately on the board's agenda to evaluate it and make a new plan. If, on the other hand, it shows up as inertia and sticking to the good old ways of working, you can reinforce it by communicating the purpose, adding resources to help develop the new ways of working and involving the relevant people so they can decide themselves on how they can contribute. Naturally, this is managed by the chairperson either by applying it on the board or by addressing the issue and providing resources to the C-level.[27]

Chapter 4

Personal Emotional Dynamics Worth Understanding

This book began by introducing the board landscape in the general sense. It was then followed by the framework of psychodynamic understanding followed by the two essential elements for building competence and confidence, agency and boundaries. We then went deeper into the details of organizational psychodynamic systems and their application to boards. In this and the following chapter, we will explore these concepts further.

Previously, you became acquainted with the concepts of board dynamics both in the goal-rational field where roles, boundaries and regulations are formally defined, and in the psychodynamic field, where all the preconscious and unconscious elements come into play. To deepen your knowledge in the psychodynamic field, this chapter presents basic mechanisms to help you become conscious of human behavior. These mechanisms are the basis for the dynamics of the board, but they may be difficult to understand at first glance. However, note that they apply in your own backyard, in the group space as well as in the outside world.

In this chapter, you will be introduced to four psychological elements: anxiety, projection, transference and countertransference.

By getting a better understanding of these elements, you will be able to recognize how these psychological elements can manifest in the board's leadership dynamics. You will be more adept at analyzing the situation and accessing the state of a board meeting when progress stalls or there is a negative atmosphere. For example, you may be able to predict or see why board members suddenly stop coming, are delayed or are passive in meetings. Many things play out under the surface in the boardroom.

The better your lens on these elements, the better you understand your own actions and the more grounded you will be. In this chapter, you will gain the tools to tolerate crises, conflicts and bad manners without acting out and, as such, stay focused on the target.

PERSPECTIVE

∽୭° The Importance of Understanding Personal Emotional Dynamics

Understanding the dynamics below the surface and the regression pressure between the goal-rational field and the psychodynamic field requires grasping several key psychological elements.

You could study all aspects of psychology, but when applying psychodynamic organizational concepts to boards, we will focus on just enough elements to get your feet wet. These elements derive from the theory of psychoanalysis by Freud and are focused primarily on processes which, broadly stated, are mental activities occurring without awareness.[28] [29]

First of all, what is behind unconscious processes? This was touched upon in previous chapters, but you are now going to get a more nuanced view of what could be affecting behavior on the board. Recognizing the role of unconscious motives and emotions makes you more capable of recognizing the influence these have on the board's dynamics. This gives you insight into how the board works and how you function as a board member.

Secondly, examining interpersonal relationships helps you to get beyond appearances so that you can understand how past experiences shape current relational dynamics and organizational culture. What we bring with us from past relationships, be it five minutes ago or as far back as childhood, affects the board from the minute we gather together.

Thirdly, defense mechanisms are worth taking a look at. They may hinder progress in board work, manifesting in obstacles that stall making a final decision or adopting new strategic areas. Defense mechanisms are both social defenses and coping mechanisms. They are used by both individuals and groups to manage anxiety and stress.

Finally, looking at recurring patterns in interpersonal relationships may also shed some light on why a certain behavior is present in the board. All board members carry early life experiences formed with significant others, such as caregivers. These experiences form deeply ingrained desires, needs and goals that shape their personalities. In adulthood, and therefore, on the board as well, these recurring patterns can be seen as predictable relationship patterns. They may manifest themselves in the way the chair runs the meeting, for example. According to how the chairperson's family structure was set up and how they were controlled or allowed to explore as a child, the chair may see control as a way of managing the board meeting. Patterns such as these influence how we interact with others, which could lead to conflicts or misunderstandings if not addressed.

For these reasons, understanding the underlying psychological elements can help you analyze the behavior on the board as a group and what part you and each board member play in these interactions.

PITFALLS

Pay Attention When Analyzing Personal Emotional Dynamics

In the previous chapter, you were presented with possible pitfalls you may encounter when considering psychodynamics. It is important to emphasize that, with so many psychological elements and situations to contemplate, you could end up being too focused on the psychodynamic field and take up too much of the board's or chairperson's time.

The psychological elements explained here are based on research of clinical observations made on people with serious mental issues, which therefore may exaggerate the observed behaviors. Each individual is unique, so despite some universal psychological knowledge, the interpretation must not be seen as the truth. The psychodynamic approach may fail to capture key issues in the structure of the board, including formal roles, responsibilities and organization.[30]

More specifically, the risk of working with psychodynamics is that it may result in misinterpretations that bring a false foundation for decision-making. Members may feel overwhelmed on a private and personal level. This could disturb the focus on the task at hand for particular members.

What You Need to Know

Many elements affect the dynamics of the board. This section discusses the ones most touched upon by the literature on psychodynamics. The psychological elements below are also what I have seen as most common in the boardroom, probably as a result of conscious observation. These elements are anxiety, transference, countertransference and projections. They are closely related, but the differences will be explained so that you can make better use of each element and grasp the nuances of board dynamics.[31]

Anxiety

Working on a task may be rewarding and fill you with joy if what you are doing makes sense to you. Its purpose supports your own purpose in life, that of creating something, making money and helping people. But to work on a task involves feelings, which means there is a possibility of provoking the feeling of anxiety.

Anxiety is an emotional state of uneasiness and worry. It is viewed not only as a signal of danger in the outside world, but can indicate unconscious conflicts and unresolved issues. In a boardroom environment, this anxiety may be based on three different fears.

First is the fear of not being up to resolving the problem. You may say to yourself, "I cannot do the job that I am here to do." This may come up when the board processes subjects that are not in your area of expertise.

Second, there is the fear that others will not approve of your proposed solution or how you would like it to be carried out. On the board, this could happen when you wish to bring your main competencies into play, but no one else understands your field.

Finally, there is the fear of being "too much" and being excluded from the group. This is a common feeling in a board where members may feel like they ask too many questions.

It may also be caused if the task itself is dangerous. For example, you may be working on the board of a company in a financial crisis and are headed for bankruptcy. Or you may be on the board of a catastrophe aid organization like Doctors Without Borders.

Even within the primary task of the board lies a potential provocation of anxiety. The board must control and correct the operational organization if it does not comply with regulations. Or they may have to fire the CEO if they do not do their job or refuse to comply with the strategy, values or legal requirements set by the board. Tasks like these may send each board member into their own vulnerabilities, such as exclusion from the group, losing family income, being exposed as incompetent etc.

Anxiety may cause a person to stop working on the task at hand or avoid it by working on other tasks. For example, if the CEO is not performing well in their organizational leadership role and it is difficult to address the problem, the chairperson may focus more on the financial performance of the company. Or, the board may prefer to expand on the areas where the CEO is successful because the board may be conflict-averse, and then the group follows the chair.

If you feel your heart beat faster, are distracted from the meeting, are dwelling on other members' appearance more than on the subject at hand or are simply waiting for the chairperson or other authority to take action, you may be experiencing some kind of anxiety. The entire group may fall into these patterns. So, look up and explore whether it is your own anxiety, someone else's, the whole group's anxiety or simply the fact that the topic or situation is threatening to the company.[32]

Projection

Projection is a defense mechanism where a person applies their own current inner experience onto another person because it is too difficult, painful or shameful to consciously deal with. In other words, projection serves as a way to protect oneself from uncomfortable emotions or aspects of the self by externalizing them onto others.[33]

The board is a semi-temporary organization and a breeding ground for projections. Everybody comes from other organizations, other places and other boards, bringing with them their own family structures. So, you may bring on feelings from outside which may appear during meetings. These are not easy to spot due to the short time board members are together throughout the year.

To give a simple example, let's say you just came from a really positive and innovative meeting where your ideas were heard and you were given royal treatment. You may bring this energy with you and project your own excitement onto other people in the room because it may be too overwhelming or "unprofessional" to be so happy. Conversely, let's say your last meeting was terrible. You feel like you were hit by a truck. You feel sad and powerless. When you have difficulty carrying these emotions, you may project shame onto others to make it bearable for you. For instance, if you are tired, you may greet a member by saying, "Hi, Agnes. Good to see you. How are you? You look tired. Are you okay?" In short, where you come from comes with you to the board room.

You can say that projection is a survival mechanism; a way to not have to feel or bear your own feelings. If you are brought up in an environment where you were not allowed to express anger, especially towards authority figures, then anger may be a feeling you cannot express unless you are really outraged. To survive the feeling of anger, you end up pushing the buttons of other people so that they get angry. This is projection and you may invoke that dynamic at every meeting.

Projections may also work as a group thinking of external groups; for instance, the "terrible competitor."

To add another dimension, a projection may play out as a projective identification, which is where the recipient of the projection may unconsciously adopt the projected traits as their own. This leads to a complex interplay between the projector and the recipient. In the example above, the other person may actually start feeling tired.

Looking out for projections and projective identifications, both your own and that of others towards you, strengthens you against taking on other people's feelings. This permits you to be present with your own feelings and be accountable for them.[34]

Transference

Transference is an unconscious way of redirecting your feelings and attitudes from past relationships onto a new person. It is how you show up in a group based on your past experiences. If your family life was filled with tough authority behavior from your parents, then you may take this way of working into the board room. You may treat the chairperson as someone who cannot be questioned. Or you may be afraid that the chairperson will stop you from expressing your views and feelings. This behavior will rob you of the influence you are meant to have, hindering you from taking on your responsibility as a full-blown board member.

A board holds the overall power of the business and has the overarching authority to make decisions. These relationships and power dynamics on the board may provide a good breeding ground for transference.

One example is a member who, at every board meeting, speaks highly of the chairperson. It is as if the flattery is a part of being seen and earning the trust of the board management. If this thesis is valid, it may be a case of transference from a childhood where that person only got attention from his or her parents by being nice and speaking highly of them. It could have been a family with many children in which there was a lot of noise, many daily tasks and it was a constant struggle to get the attention of the parents.[35]

Countertransference

Countertransference is when one person's reenactment of their own childhood patterns in the present organization causes someone else in the group to engage them and play out the expected dynamic transferred from childhood. Countertransference is narrowly defined as a specific reaction to someone else's transference and works much in the same way as transference.

If you take the time to explore and acknowledge your own behavior, awareness of countertransference dynamics on the board makes you conscious of your relationship with the other members. It is not easy to distinguish between your own feelings, your own transference and interacting with others as a response to their transference.

In the example earlier, the board member who was always praising the chairperson could be flattered and may give the board member a special status in the meeting, just like parents who favor one child over another. It could be that the chairperson takes pleasure in this relationship. In this case, the chair is engaging in countertransference.[36]

Understanding the Difference Between Projection, Transference, and Countertransference

It may seem like projections, transference, and countertransference are almost the same thing. But in boardroom exploration, it is valuable to see the difference. You need to be able to react accordingly because your own reactions are different depending on the background of the defense.

Projection is a form of protection and a way of externalizing your inner experience in the *here and now* (which you cannot keep to yourself) onto other people. You can project the feelings in the room, on social media or if you text or post at a meeting.

Transference is a parallel shifting of your inner system *from the past* onto the boardroom environment in order to meet your need for familiarity. That goes for whatever was familiar to you in childhood, be it living with a patriarchal parent, being the youngest sibling, having an over-caring parent or being a part of a very democratic family structure.

There is both positive and negative transference. In therapy, the therapist and the client can do a lot of good work together through positive transference without addressing it, but you have to do something about the negative transference.

Countertransference is when you react to another person's transference to you, bringing forth your past system into the present board room and *reenacting with you in your parallel processing* of old patterns. It may roll out as an interaction with a former co-worker which both of you interpret as a conflict because you were both raised to be the alpha and take control.

For instance, at one board meeting, a member who had experienced sexism aggressively disagreed with someone who had made a comment they deemed sexist. It could become a projection if the board member is unable to bear the emotion and projects their anger to another board member. Or the board member may respectfully voice their observation that the power balance is not as it usually is and respect is lacking. You can tell the difference between the two by noticing if the board member has agency and does not impose their emotions on other people in the room.

In general, projection involves attributing one's own feelings here and now to others, while transference involves redirecting past feelings onto someone in the present. Both concepts are important in understanding human behavior. When the person experiencing transference reacts with his or her own feelings, it is countertransference.[37]

When you work on a board with the primary task of ensuring the particular business' finances and compliance with regulations, patterns such as projection, transference and countertransference may not surface immediately. But over time, transference and countertransference are sure to happen. Observe and explore them so you can comprehend why the board work sometimes is not efficient, or you get a strange remark or are put down for being a minority.

What You Need to Do

It is important to get acquainted with psychological elements and the situations where they play out in order to understand the dynamics of the organization. It is not straightforward, but this section lists some questions and suggestions to help familiarize you with them.

Anxiety

Test yourself out and your own anxiety triggers by noting when your mind wanders or your heart races for the duration of a week. For instance, when reading the newspaper, when you're afraid of not being able to solve the task at hand or when you're afraid of a lack of commitment or connection.

Are you already aware of or have you noticed any anxiety patterns in your own life? Did you notice anyone else's anxiety and what caused it?

Whenever you feel anxious, take 30 seconds and place your feet flat on the ground, close your eyes and breathe deeply three times. This technique can be used to ground yourself, in general. To assist the group, you may want to express that the current topic is hard to work with. Your awareness could also ground the group.

Projection

Use the profiling from Chapter 6 to understand yourself. Recall past situations when you felt overwhelmed by a feeling and did not understand where it came from.

Check with the board to see which feelings are expressed. Those that are not are most likely to be projected onto other people in the room. You may place yourself in a consultant's role and look at the board and how behaviors play out. Make your own thesis about the undercurrents on the board to understand and be better prepared to work in that environment.

Do you see authority-pleasing board members as described earlier in the chapter? You may be triggered by this because it shifts power and may cause the chairperson to ignore other members who are not flattering them. In this kind of situation, you could say, "I agree with Peter that our chair Marie is doing a great job and I also think that every one of us is doing a great job too, all chipping in with our own expertise." In this way, you do not put down the complimentary board member, but you equalize their statements by praising the whole group.

At the same time, this brings with it the risk of not directly addressing the elephant in the room.

Transference and Countertransference

Analyze your family structure. How did power play out? How did you get attention? What was most important? How did your parents interact with you and your siblings? How did you interact with your siblings?

Look at your professional life. Do you see any patterns from your childhood?

In the boardroom, do you experience a shifting power system that does not align with official roles? Who gets to speak the most? How do you earn your rights? If you see a misaligned power structure, you may support the people who are not speaking or have an offline chat with the chairperson.

A part of psychologists' and psychotherapists' work includes avoiding entering into negative countertransference, so they attend supervision and therapy sessions regularly so that they can be mindful of their own themes and background feelings. This is something you can do as well.

You may start noting your feelings and learn about your themes and underlying feelings. What is difficult for you and what is not? Whatever they are, if they are difficult to talk about, they may be attached to shame, which could often be expressed as unconscious behavior.

Understanding the Difference Between Projection, Transference, and Countertransference

Differentiate between the feelings you recognize from your past systems, like your family structure or previous jobs, and what feelings are part of the here and now. Do you have a feeling from a situation that just occurred? For example, someone told a sad story. Then, identify which feelings are reactions towards other people's feelings in the room.

From the above list of actions, choose the areas most relevant to you and to the board you are applying them to. Nobody does it perfectly. Perfection is to be agile and to react to stagnation. But by being aware of all these elements and knowing what to do, you have the tools necessary to support yourself, when needed.

How to Recover

As with all psychology, you must be aware that the analysis you do is an interpretation from your point of view based upon models of understanding. As mentioned above, this could lead to pitfalls. You need to come back when you end up in a complicated situation where you may have missed out on some information.

Always be open to feedback on your reflections so you can modify your understanding of the dynamics or explore further. In case the subject of psychodynamics is overwhelming for the board, you have to step back and let the chairperson manage the board to get back on track. Communicating your findings when receiving the feedback helps you support the chairperson in bringing the board back on track.

The board may also get professional guidance in case the situation gets stuck. This is similar to the guidance the board may seek on regulatory issues or other tangible areas where expertise is needed.

Chapter 5

Core Group Dynamics Worth Understanding

In the previous chapter, you were introduced to four psychological elements: anxiety, transference, countertransference and projections. In this chapter, you will find a description of different core group dynamics in which personal emotional dynamics unfold. You will learn about areas such as the projective room, basic assumption groups, biases – diversity, relations and roles, loyalty to different organizations and finally, trust in the boardroom.

By getting a better understanding of how these dynamics function in different settings, you will be even more adept at analyzing the situation and accessing the state of a board meeting when progress stalls or there is a negative atmosphere. For example, you may be able to see with more precision why the board is not working on the primary task. Many things play out under the surface in the boardroom. Here, you will further fine-tune your instruments and find even more serenity. This chapter adds to the tools you have already earned so that you can handle crises, conflicts and bad manners with composure and thus, stay on task.

⌒○ The Importance of Understanding Core Group Dynamics

To get an even deeper understanding of group dynamics below the surface and the regression pressure between the goal-rational field and the psychodynamic field, we will look into some concepts of how the dynamics in groups may play out.

While you could study all aspects of organizational psychology, in this chapter we are looking at how to apply psychodynamic organizational concepts to boards. Therefore, we will look at just a few elements as an introduction to the psychodynamic field.

Generally speaking, understanding the core group dynamics is crucial for boards because they significantly influence decision-making and overall board effectiveness.

Unconscious processes were touched upon in the previous chapters, but here you will get a more nuanced view of what could be affecting group behavior on the board. Recognizing the role of unconscious motives and emotions makes you more capable of seeing the influence these have on the board's dynamics. This gives you an insight into how the board works and how you function as a board member.

Core group dynamics can have both a positive and negative effect on interpersonal relations. Embracing diversity has proven, as we saw in the introduction, to enhance decision quality by incorporating varied perspectives into the boardroom. Working with trust and loyalty in the boardroom supports members so that they can act in the best interest of the organization that they serve.

By managing the core group dynamics, you can encourage collaboration, effective governance and open communication, all of which can free the core dynamics of any hindrances in the boardroom.

For these reasons, understanding the group dynamics together with the personal emotional dynamics can help you analyze the behavior of the board as a group as well as what part each board member plays in these interactions.

PITFALLS

Pay Attention When Analyzing Core Group Dynamics

In the previous chapter, you were presented with possible pitfalls that you may encounter when considering personal emotional dynamics. When looking at core group dynamics, there are also quite a few psychological elements to consider. Be aware of becoming overly attentive to psychodynamics as it can be time-consuming for the board or the chairperson.

Keep in mind that the psychological concepts presented here are derived from clinical work and, as such, are based on the behaviors of people with serious mental issues. We draw from studies of this clinical work to crystalize elements that are present in groups, albeit in a less extreme manner.

When it comes to core group dynamics, pay special attention to the idea that mismanagement of psychodynamic elements may cause conflicts and miscommunications in the boardroom. Unrecognized group behaviors such as ignoring biases may lead to unproductive decision-making. Lack of clarity in roles and relations may result in power struggles and lack of accountability. Loyalty conflicts and lack of trust in the board may compromise objectivity and lead to ineffective governance.

What You Need to Know

Many theorists research how organizations work and how to lead them, while consultants have developed models based on various organizational theories. In the following section, you will find a collection of material that may help you understand the dynamics of a board, both for yourself and for the actions of the other members. Being conscious of these factors will prepare you for situations that could occur in your board work. Many situations could be relevant to you. The following is a compilation that I have chosen, based on my experience as a board member, and as such are my priorities. Listing them down here, they are projective room and projective identification, basic assumption groups, biases - diversity, relations and roles, loyalty to different organizations and trust.

Projective Rooms

People fantasize. When people are excluded from a room, a place, a community or a virtual community, fantasies thrive. You may be familiar with the term FOMO – Fear Of Missing Out. This is part of the feeling we, as human beings, have when we are not part of a group and cannot see what is happening.

We talk about the projective room both physically and psychologically. For instance, in 1990, a worldwide IT company declared an open-door policy. Up until that point, all doors to offices had been closed, especially the doors to the managers' offices. This meant that the managers had been missing out on the opportunity to sense what was going on in the organization. In the meantime, the employees had been developing fantasies about what the managers were planning to do with their work lives. Some employees started to "calendar surf" by comparing which meetings people attended or when a "secret" spot was occupied on the calendar.

Psychologically speaking, you could also talk about a closed door and a closed room. Today, our virtual societies and meetings are food for fantasies and as such, a place for projecting your inner wishes, fears and anxieties.

Knowing that projective rooms can materialize at any time, you may want to be conscious of the room's existence, of the fantasies about the rooms you are in, those which are closed from others, and about the rooms that are closed to you. Some rooms could be your own operational organization, your other boards, the committees on the board and the fact that the board is closed to the organization. To avoid the creation of projective rooms, you may consider voicing to others which room you are coming from when you give input at the board meeting. For example:

"As a representative coming directly from our recent city council meeting, I want to share an important update for transparency and collaboration. One of the key topics we discussed and made decisions on was cybersecurity protection for municipal systems. Given its relevance to our shared objectives, I thought it would be helpful to briefly outline what was decided and how it aligns with our broader agenda. My goal is to ensure everyone here is informed and has the opportunity to provide input or raise any concerns as we move forward together."

Additionally, your awareness of your imagination about rooms that are closed to you can help you react consciously and allow you to bring up your ideas if you find them relevant to the subject at hand. Let's say you are discussing hiring a new CEO and a committee has been established to find this person and present them to the board for final approval. You may have feelings and fantasies about the candidate presented and what went on during the selection process. You may have liked to ask the following questions: "What was the process like in the committee? What discrepancies did you have? What were the outlier opinions? What were you most aligned on? What did the second candidate lack?"

The "board's own time" during a meeting is also a projective room for the CEO and the rest of the operational organization. It can awaken feelings in the people from the organization when they are asked to leave. Some years back, "the board's own time" was not even an item on the board meeting agenda. When it was applied, it took a lot of time to reassure the CEO and to clarify that this was a boundary. If the board does not have a moment for itself, it tends to melt into the executive board (C-level management.). This makes it difficult to take on the primary task if you do not have these boundaries. It sets a boundary between the board and the operational organization, showing that the board has the overall responsibility of the organization. If the board members have conflicts or need to discuss processes, for example, it is necessary to keep this space reserved for the board only.

The chairperson should manage this boundary and ensure that both the board and the operational organization feel safe and have closure at the end of the board meeting. This could be done by having everyone from the operational organization enter the room again, by saying goodbye, leaving the papers on the table or staying in the room while the people trickle out. However, there was one board where some of the C-level were so anxious and angry about "the board's own time" that they left the premises with only a halfhearted goodbye. On another board, all the people from the organization left for a while and waited until "the board's own time" was over and then came back for small talk and one-on-one planning. The latter situation provided a fruitful closure for everyone.

As you can see, the dynamics of the projective room clearly have its foundation in the concept of projection, which is the way we as human beings deal with curiosity and difficult and shameful feelings.

Basic Assumption Groups

When boards are working on the primary task, we use the terminology "work group" as defined by Bion.[38] Work group dynamics according to Bion are rational, task-focused group dynamics where members collaborate effectively to achieve a clear goal. It emphasizes productivity, openness and shared responsibility.

As opposed to the work group dynamics, the basic assumption group dynamics are unconscious, emotionally driven dynamics where anxiety disrupts the group's purpose. Members may exhibit dependency, avoidance or irrational behaviors, prioritizing emotional needs over tasks.

The loss of a sense of purpose may cause the board to stop working on the primary task. For example, the two parts of the primary task (optimizing for both shareholders and the operational organization) could oppose each other. Another possibility could be that the purpose of the semi-temporary organization is blurry because of relatively rare interactions during the year. When you do not meet often and have other boards and organizations, you may mentally mix them and have another agenda that you bring with you. For instance, the board may have appointed members who come with an agenda from their home organization. Some democratically elected members may want to enter a board so that they can emphasize their own special requests; for example, a customer-elected member who had problems with the organization's products, or an employee-elected member who does not agree with the company's personnel policies and other similar elected-member foci.

The board may stop working on the primary task if it does not understand or see its role and the task at hand. For example, if the organization does not work on the core business, this puts the board and the organization out of sync. Or if not all board members are active but are still made accountable and responsible for what is decided or happening on the board.

In case the board loses sight of the primary task and meaning, the group may fall into the state of a basic assumption and inadvertently start working on other tasks that still make sense but are not the main objective.39 You have probably seen this in various places in your life because it occurs any time people are together: in families, at kindergarten, in line at the supermarket, in business groups or at a social event where you do not have anything in common but you've been put at the same table. In that situation, you may see that two people start talking and the rest just listen.

The concept of basic assumption groups is a way to understand the dynamics of group behavior. These groups operate at an unconscious level and impact how a group functions or not.

Dependency

In this state, the group is highly dependent on the leader of the group. The members do not seem to have agency and seek guidance, comfort and sustenance from the leader. The group seems passive and relies on authority. On a board, that could mean highly controlled leadership by the chairperson or a case where the CEO runs the board.

Pairing

In this state, the group reacts to a meaningless topic by listening to two members of the group discussing or interacting. The subject could be either something relevant to the group or out of context. In both situations, the rest of the members do not interact because the discussion does not make sense to them. They simply wait. By permitting the two parties to live out the interaction, the rest of the members are hoping that it will save the group. Thus, there may be emotional attachment and idealization. For example, it could unfold as a debate between two members on a board where the rest of the members do not know about the technology, such as a debate about the ethics of generative AI on the board of a carpentry business, where generative AI is not taken into consideration. The board may be shifting focus instead of addressing the difficulty of a financial crisis and the likely scenario of letting people go.

Fight-Flight

This group state is the most well-known. It is part of many people's general understanding of how we, as human beings, may react to unpleasant situations. When the purpose of the group's work is not apparent, it is mortally threatening and generates anxiety. In this state, the flight reaction is to avoid talking about the problem at hand and talk about something different. The fight reaction is to cause a confrontation of any kind, either inside or outside the group. Instead of passively listening to two board members, the board could become aggressive towards the tax authorities who (in the minds of the basic assumption group) caused the financial crisis by collecting due taxes. A more productive response would be for the board to park the problem with the CFO to figure out whether the tax authorities are right and then move on according to the agenda of the board meeting.

Remember that these basic assumption groups influence group behavior and can shift over time as the group's focus changes.

Biases

People are biased. As such, we may be blind to input from differently minded individuals. You may say, "I am not racist, sexist or ageist or affected by any other kind of bias." But in reality, we all have biases because we need this mechanism to survive. The alternative would be to investigate and analyze the totality of information we are exposed to, which is not possible. The advantage of biases is that they speed up any scrutiny, rapid decision-making, or creation of motivation that you may need to do.[40]

The dark side of biases is that you may only hear and understand what you expect the person to say and do. One common bias is related to gender. The first person you met in life was your mother, who carried you and nursed you as a vulnerable baby. In your adult life, this may translate into the assumption that all women are caring and nursing. So, when women on boards then play hardball and do not assume the caretaker part, they are seen as not fulfilling their below-the-surface role.

Likewise, you may be young, but people on the board are older. This could make it difficult for you to be heard and respected. They may think you do not have enough life experience or that you do not know about board work. These biases could prevent them from regarding your input as relevant or considering you as competent. In this case, preparation is your platform for demanding your rights and taking up your space so that you can fulfill the responsibility you have taken and has been given to you by entering the board.

Biases are of major importance in today's diverse boards. Years back, boards were more homogeneous. Today, it is part of good governance to seek out a diverse board in all aspects, going beyond professional background. Diversity includes gender, age, race, geography, experience, political background, religion, social background etc. When you go from a homogeneous group to a diverse group, all your biases will rise and you may be anxious about the unknown. The chairperson needs to manage this situation both by leading the meeting and being aware of their own biases.

At my first board meeting for a technical company (elected by the customers), I was most likely regarded as an "angry female customer" who did not have a clue of what board work was all about nor what the business was all about. The latter was correct. However, I had been running a career as a board professional for many years and had already taken organizations through tough crises as a chairperson. This expectation of the part I would play could have come from the previous person in this role. How did the former member behave? What was this person's personal authority etc? In addition, I am a woman. What were the board's biases concerning gender? Maybe they had ideas such as, "She's just a woman", "too many feelings", "too young", "nice to have someone to project feelings onto" etc. Below the surface, the role some members could be expecting was not at all what I do as a female board professional. In a scenario like this, it may take time and be a struggle to get recognition for this position.

You may find many biases on a board and I have seen different biases play out throughout my board experience. Listed below are some that would be helpful to understand in a boardroom setting.[41]

- **Anchoring bias.** To be convinced by the first information you receive, which also confirms the conviction you already held. Any other information is reduced to the same convention. This bias may get you stuck in methods and hinder innovation.

- **Apophenia.** To seek meaning in something that does not have any or see patterns where they do not exist. This is important when looking for below-the-surface currents. If you are always seeking patterns, you may become biased and susceptible, and believe that random events influence future outcomes (the gambler's fallacy).

- **Confirmation bias.** This is the same mechanism as anchoring. But rather than being based on data, it is related to beliefs. It can lead to tunnel vision and prevent you from considering alternative viewpoints. This is also very important when you explore the psychodynamic field.

- **Hindsight bias.** This bias is where you believe that you knew the outcome of the situation beforehand, which then distorts your judgment and your impression of self-reliance. You may hear yourself saying something like, "What did I tell you?"

- **Availability heuristic.** You may be biased about your evaluation of risk and future scenarios. This bias is based on how easily you can recall a similar event. For instance, you can readily remember having a CEO resign and it was recurrent. Therefore, you may see this as likely to happen again.

- **Sunk-cost fallacy.** If you have invested resources in developing a new product with a new strategy, it may be difficult to let go if the market or technology has changed. You then tend to find arguments to continue the development. But here lies a paradox: In start-up companies, "crazy" ideas that stick around for a long time may look like a dead end. Likewise, a particular idea may be the dream of the founder and therefore, they continue to push it because they cannot let it go.

- **Gender bias.** While this is called gender bias, it covers all biases related to experiences, culture, and personal beliefs. Biases related to gender, race, religion, age, geography, place in society, education, line of business, physical appearance, etc make you expect that a person will say a certain thing, act a certain way, or take on predicted invisible roles. This bias prevents you from listening to other board members with an open mind.

Being aware of your biases, both data- and sentiment-driven, makes you more open to other people's input. It makes the board a place for generating ideas and, as such, for creating value for stakeholders and the organization.

Challenging your own biases is essential to creating an inclusive mindset. To become aware of your biases, there are many ways to tame your inner beast. Dealing with others' biases towards you is important so that you can show up with confidence and competency, hold your stance and feel your feet on the ground. Remember, you cannot change people. You can only change yourself, your behavior and how you receive input from others.

To address how people are biased towards you, you first need to spot the bias. Some are easy to find, such as a man opening the door for a woman entering the boardroom as a gentlemanly gesture. Anybody in the room can recognize this as male/female positioning. You, as a person, could make sure to distance yourself from this role by refraining from entering the room the next time. Other biases are very subtle. To pick up on these, you have to mentally step out of the room and away from the interactions from time to time during the board meeting so that you can look at the dynamics.

Biases are the basis of a great deal of the dynamics in the boardroom. By being aware and mitigating your own biases, you can be a more competent board member. Being aware of other members' biases towards you gives you the opportunity to counteract them. You can do this by taking up the problem during "the board's own time" slot, by acting differently, by wearing a different outfit or by presenting yourself with dignity and taking your responsibility seriously. Taking actions like these helps you to show up more confidently in the boardroom.

Relations and Roles

Another topic that affects board dynamics is relations and roles. You have already been introduced to these elements at the beginning of the previous chapter and also in this chapter, in which you were presented with some examples of how relations and roles impact how a board works on the primary task.

The relationship between the primary task and the role you take on as a person is very important to address with yourself. Confirm that you are on this particular board for the right reasons. These reasons should be to create value for the organization and shareholders and to make sure that your values meet the organization's values and vice versa.

It's just as important to understand the connection between the primary task and the relationships on the board as it is to be conscious of this. That goes for both your interactions in the goal-rational field (previous acquaintances from both professional and private life) as well as the relations created below the surface in the psychodynamic field.

Unofficial roles on the board depend on the individual members and the group dynamics. These roles can be defined by the member's family structure, such as what your childhood family dynamic was like, your birth order (oldest, youngest, middle child etc), or how you were allowed to be present in the family (a people-pleaser, an alpha etc).

The concept of "the promoted sibling" is a psychodynamic study of how our family structure could affect how we show up in organizations. It puts a special focus on how to manage this dynamic in the organization. Why are some board members promoted by being selected for a specific task, such as a group of people tasked with hiring a new CEO? To lead a team of creative people, the chairperson has to pay attention to the relationships between leaders and followers as well as the relationships between the followers themselves.[42]

It is often difficult to see precisely, but when a crisis hits, the underlying roles, envy and fear of envy expose themselves more clearly. Once, on a board where a major crisis suddenly occurred, one of the board members became clearly defensive on behalf of the chairperson. This member took over the time management of the meeting and was aggressive towards others when they did not stick strictly to the timeline. It became a mix between a followership and a takeover which caused the dynamic of the board to change.

Loyalty to Different Organizations

On a board, it is no secret that the members have loyalties to many different organizations. Loyalty can be described as standing up for your values, sharing values and working for the organization you are part of.

Loyalty can lead to conflicts, such as choosing between being loyal to the board's primary task or being loyal to the chairperson, especially if the chairperson is not prioritizing the primary task.

I work as a consultant. So I am very familiar with the dilemma of being employed and paid by the consultancy company but solving the tasks and being more physically present at the customer's organization. You may have experienced this concerning your loyalty to the organization which employs you. For example, you work for a medical company producing anesthetics. You feel pride when you see a commercial for your company or when someone mentions that they have heard of it. In addition, you work as a volunteer at the Red Cross and you also feel loyalty towards this organization. Then, a catastrophe occurs where the Red Cross is assisting but they lack anesthetics because they are too costly. You may end up in a dilemma and you can feel your loyalty bouncing back and forth.

When working on a board, the potential for a loyalty conflict is always present. It is part of the very nature of board work to serve in several board positions and often, have an operational job as well. Before entering a board, you should ask yourself if any conflicts of interest are present and voice them. On most boards, you are required to divulge all your posts, commitments and investments. Even if it is not mandatory, do it anyway so you can be clear about your motives. The following scenarios present potential loyalty conflicts:

- Joining a start-up company in the same business area as your operational job, but probably with a different target customer.

- Joining a volunteer organization working in a field that is opposed to your operational job. For instance, working on the board of a volunteer organization that protects drinking water while working at a company that produces artificial fertilizer for the farming industry.

- Investing in shares of the company which will be overseen by the board position.

- Being on an advisory board where a crisis could affect another one of your organizations.

- Being elected as a board member by a particular group, like a political party, employees, customers, parents etc. This may motivate you to take the side of your voters and avoid taking full responsibility on the board of the organization.

Bear in mind that when you work on a particular board, you are *not* representing a group. Your goal should always be to make decisions in the company's best interests; that is, the interests of the shareholders and the operational organization.

In the psychodynamic field, you may also have loyalty clashes since you must split your attention between more than one "master." Which organization do I spend the most time thinking about when I let my thoughts drift? What do I do if I need to prepare for a board meeting but also have a presentation to make at my operational job? The only thing you can do is plan according to the calendar year. Set aside enough time to prepare for the board meetings. Make sure that you are in an operational position where you do not have too much on your plate. As such, you are flexible enough to handle extraordinary situations.

Some clashes could include having board meetings at the same time. In particular, annual report presentations are commonly at the same time of the year; crises in the general surroundings, such as a war, an epidemic or a financial crisis; and if your board position and operational job are in the same industry, you may have to discuss the same topic at the same time, such as NIS2 implementation.

In psychological terms, loyalty is a complex and multifaceted concept that manifests itself as a strong feeling of support or connection towards a task, person, group or organization. It may turn up as emotional attachment, commitment and trustworthiness.

Various factors can influence emotional attachment, including shared experiences, common values and personal connections. These attachments appear on a board after a seminar, for example, where the members have spent a considerable amount of time together and have probably had a nice dinner. Moments like these give people a chance to meet on a personal level and explore common or different values. The feeling of emotional attachment to someone or something makes us more likely to demonstrate loyalty. For instance, by offering help or being kind and reliable.

When you are loyal, you show commitment and the strength of that commitment shows through dedication. This dedication is dependent on shared goals, a sense of obligation and perceived benefits. So, for example, you may see less loyalty towards a departing board member at the end of an election term either because his or her expertise is no longer needed or the number of years of service exceeds good governance.[43]

When looking at the definition just stated, you may realize that loyalty is an important and complex aspect of your work on the board and your interactions with other boards.

Trust

In the section above, we have worked on loyalty and conflicts laterally between different organizations. In this section, we go through loyalty on the vertical axis: towards the operational organization, the C-level management, the board as an organization, the chairperson, the committees and finally, the investors or owners.

Within the board's primary task, there is a built-in paradox concerning trust. And within the trust itself, there is also a dilemma since trust does not exist until people behave as if it is already there. To give trust is to allow yourself to be vulnerable towards the people you would like to trust yourself.[44]

The board is obliged to ensure that the operational organization is implementing the strategy set by the board, running a financially healthy and compliant business, and doing all of this according to good governance. On the other hand, the boardroom and the work on the board are based upon confidence.

The chairperson must build a safe boardroom. In addition, everyone at the meeting must build a solid relationship with the chairperson, the other board members and the representatives of the operational organization. It would be utopian to have 100% trust among all members and the organization, but you still need to build a good enough and trustworthy environment.[45]

What needs to be in place is a secure space where your psychological safety is assured.

Psychological safety is a term defined by Professor Amy C. Edmondson of Harvard University as a workplace environment free from interpersonal fear. It is an unspoken belief shared by the members of a group that there is a safe space in which they can take interpersonal risks.[46]

When you are working in a psychologically safe space, your nervous system doesn't register risk. You will experience a safe boardroom as a place where you can speak up and your voice is valued, you feel secure enough to be honest and candid, you can share ideas, ask questions and offer comments, and you feel safe enough to make mistakes and conflicts are dealt with in a respectful manner.

To be in a safe place requires board members who act appropriately and take the responsibility that their role defines, are thoughtful and considerate and are productive and professional. To get to this stage on a board, it is highly recommended that all the above personal explorations are done constantly. In this way, you come prepared, capable and sure of yourself.[47]

The dilemma is that to promote trust in the room, you have to show trust and vulnerability. But to supervise, you need to "mistrust" what is presented. So, what do you do? You have to find the balance within yourself.

In board work, this dilemma is one of the most difficult dynamics to deal with because they are contradictory. To create trust you have to show trust. But to fulfill your role as supervisor, you have to question the trust to make sure that it is intact.

As a general rule of thumb, you can deal with this paradox by voicing the difficulty. Often, this releases the anger caused by being supervised. Another way to find balance is to both express the areas you are happy with and then ask questions about the areas where you lack the information you need to feel confident.

However, a word of caution: Make sure you are authentic when you express your contentment. The reason for this is that many people have adopted the behavior of thanking the person for the presentation and then shooting them down afterward. The person receiving the feedback may not have integrated the positive comments because it was followed by major criticism.

To illustrate how these dynamics may play out, consider the following:

A conflict in management in one particular organization surfaced, little by little. It was an old, well-established organization that, after a growth period, faced challenges internally with the change of the CEO and externally with the COVID pandemic and subsequent energy crisis. The executive management split in two, causing the organizational management to divide. However, one side was not allowed to voice their opinion. The board became deeply involved and step by step, the board was also split. Soon rumors begin to fly throughout the whole organization. It was a worrisome situation that needed intervention to release the stalled management. Fortunately, the organization was able to continue focusing on the primary task. Relief came not from the elimination of the initial causes of the split. It was, in fact, when the board came together and talked about all the lies, fears and mistrust.

Then, the board was able to go back to working on their primary task of ensuring a continuing organization, controlling the finances and setting the strategy going forward.

In a crisis like the one above, triggers are activated in each board member and it is likely that they regress to childhood or family patterns. This is where you can see how biases with diversity, childhood obstruction against authority, hunger for needs being met, fear of losing connection, lack of board structure, hunger for attention, need for performance, lack of agency and lack of trust all come to the surface.

What You Need to Do

It is important to get acquainted with psychological elements and the situations where they play out to understand the dynamics of the organization. It is not straightforward, but this section lists some questions and suggestions to help get you familiar with them.

Projective Room

Do you see any groupings, physical rooms, sub-groupings or committees that are closed to the point that you start fantasizing about what is happening in them? Do you notice others asking about your own committee work and the like? Then it would be best to start asking about what is happening in the group and start sharing about your own committee work.

A simple test to see how projective rooms work is to go stand in front of a closed door. You are probably relaxed if it is a room you know and nobody is in there. But you still may be a bit alert because you may have already experienced a door opening when you did not expect it. Then stand in front of the closed door of a room about which you know nothing. All you can do is imagine this room. You may then start thinking, feeling and fantasizing about who is in there, what they do and why you are not with them. You may be cautious and think, "When does the door open and what will happen?"

Basic Assumption Groups

Identify the state of the group by checking in with yourself and what you are experiencing. Are you bored? Do you see only two members that are active? Does it seem like the chairperson is suddenly being idolized? Or do you find that some members have become quiet while others have begun arguing heavily, with very strong opinions? In cases like these, you could verify if the board is actually working on the primary task or if it makes sense for all members to be working on the board.

You may ask the group: "What are we really trying to achieve here? Could we stop for a second to align? I have lost sight of why we are working on this matter." If the board is not mature enough to deal with such a question, you may debrief your chairperson.

Biases – Diversity

Here are steps you can take to spot your own biases and learn how to deal with them:

- **Self-reflection.** Take time. You should reflect on your beliefs, assumptions and reactions.

- **Educate yourself.** Keep learning your whole life: You should dig into cultures, identities and perspectives by interacting, reading books, watching documentaries and showing empathy. Expose yourself to diversity. You may attend workshops or go with a group of colleagues to become aware of and mitigate biases. Always stay curious about other people and engage in conversations.

- **Listen and learn.** If you are lucky enough to have someone point out your biases, listen attentively without being defensive.

- **Seek feedback.** Reach out to anyone towards whom you could be biased and to people you can trust to give you respectful feedback on how they see you.

- **Challenge your own assumptions.** Take a minute to pause instead of always charging full speed ahead. Whenever you catch yourself making assumptions, pause and question them. Are they based on evidence or stereotypes? Challenge these automatic thoughts. You may notice these assumptions by paying attention to your language and behavior. Always adjust if you find yourself assuming or talking and behaving inappropriately based on biases.

- **Challenging biases is an ongoing process.** Be patient with yourself, stay open-minded and commit to continuous learning.

- **Spot the bias within someone else.** If you have an odd feeling about something, you should note it down and spend some time looking into what is at stake. Do you see a pattern forming over time – a bias? Does it matter? Or does it prevent you from contributing to the board's primary task?

- **If bias is a problem for you, the answer is, as always, the same: Voice it.** Be careful to mention it in a respectful manner by expressing who you are and what you stand for. Set your boundaries instead of making yourself a victim who just talks about his or her needs. If you express your needs and they are not fulfilled, you may be even more frustrated and it could weaken your voice on the board. If you state your limits, you will also have to defend them when they are crossed. You may have to vote against a measure, exit or stop the discussion, leave the room or ultimately leave the board. Make sure to take these actions when you are grounded and not overwhelmed by your own feelings.

Relations and Roles

Spot your own pre-programmed structure based on your childhood by taking a look back: What was the organization like in my family? Who had the last word? Where am I in the birth order? How was I allowed to show up? How did we, as children, get attention? And more questions along that vein.

From the exploration of your family structure, move on to exploring how you show up in a professional organization. Do I emulate my family structure? Where does it work and where does it not work?

Look at the structure and dynamics of the board. Do you see any family structures being recreated? What happens? Does it work or is it hindering progress on the primary task?

If you have an issue that prevents progress and the board is mature enough, voice the stagnation during "the board's own time." Otherwise, ask for a one-on-one with the chair.

To explore further, ask yourself, "Why am I on the board? Could I have my own hidden agenda that is not the board's primary task? What are we actually doing?" The board exists because we need it. What is the board's relationship to the primary task? Does it create value for the organization? You may ask yourself, "As I am new here, can I really help the board with the primary task?"

By exploring these dynamics, you may be better at navigating your role on the board and at stopping your own below-the-surface diversions. Take some time during and after the meeting to reflect upon and voice what you see. Finally, ask for feedback on your own role on the board from the chairperson. Use the board evaluation and "the board's own time" to bring forward observations. In case the board is not mature enough to discuss these areas, you can use the observations as information on the landscape you are working in. This will make you feel sure of yourself and your capacities so that you can bring your knowledge and experience forward in a professional manner. It also creates an opening so that your internal feelings do not get in the way of a professional debate.

Loyalty to Different Organizations

Before entering a board, you should always ask yourself if any conflicts of interest are present and voice them. For most boards, you are required to present all your posts, commitments and investments. Even if it is not mandatory, do it anyway to be clear about your motives.

Find your own personal way to shift into the board mindset. You can do this by trying the following techniques.:

If you are working on something else before a board meeting, be sure to say goodbye to the people you are with, send an email saying you will be at a board meeting, or set an out-of-office message. Leave unrelated or unnecessary material – both tangible and intangible – behind so that you bring only what you need for the board meeting with you.

Before entering the boardroom, take a minute to empty your mind. Think about both the professional side and the psychological side of where you came from and what you are going to do after the meeting. Write it down on your phone or a piece of paper. Leave this in your bag and come back to it after the board meeting. Put on another outfit or you can simply take off your jacket and hang it in the closet. Don't forget to turn off your phone before entering the meeting room. Greet each person in the room. Say hello, shake hands or greet according to local cultural norms. When the board meeting is over, say goodbye, shake hands or bid farewell in the local way too.

After the meeting, empty your head by writing down your own thoughts, feelings and fantasies. Note if you recognize what emotion you transferred into the meeting (happiness, sadness, anxiety, anger etc). Notice, as well, what psychological material you are taking with you from the meeting. You may want to change back into your clothing from before and not bring the board material to the new setting you will enter after the board meeting.

<u>Trust</u>

Show your own trust in the board, the board members and the organization. Consider these questions to find your balance:

- How do you make yourself trustworthy?

- How do you express yourself through body language and voice?

- Can you trust a sweet-talking person?

- How do you promote trust in a group?

- Are you ready to take the risk of promoting trust?

To find out if you are in a safe boardroom, ask yourself the following questions:

- Do people act consistently?

- Do I hear gossip during the breaks?

- Do people dare to speak up?

- Are diverse people regarded equally?

- How do others react to me when I speak?

- Do I see any signs of narcissism or psychopathy? Meaning, does anybody avoid accountability, appear grandiose and self-centered, or do they have a tendency to twist the truth? If you see such a pattern, be alert. Most cases of fraud and mistrust on boards derive from a narcissistic CEO or chairperson.

Keep in mind that there is a dilemma between promoting trust in the room (by showing trust and being vulnerable) and control, where you need to "mistrust" what is presented. Therefore, you must present feedback in a balanced way and be respectful of other people.

From the above list of actions, choose the areas that are most relevant to you and to the board you are applying them to. Nobody does it perfectly. Perfection is to be agile and to react to stagnation. But by being aware of all these elements and knowing what to do, you have the tools necessary to support yourself.

How to Recover

Failures when working with core group dynamics and psychodynamics, in general, require the chairperson's interaction and management of the meeting. However, you as an individual member may always have choices to make. In the sections above, you were presented with various actions to take and one general action is to voice what you encounter in a respectful manner. Or, if the board is not in a place where this is possible or there is no time for the debate, talk to the chairperson after the meeting.

Concerning basic assumption groups specifically, it is worth mentioning that when you see the board is heading into or is already in a basic assumption phase, be aware. No matter how much you try to stay on the subject, it will be difficult for the board to get back to the primary task.

Turn your frustration into curiosity and ask, "What are we really trying to achieve? Could we take a moment to align? I have lost sight of why we are discussing this matter in the first place." If the board is not mature enough to deal with such a question, you may want to debrief your chairperson.

For long-term development, your board may look into growing awareness capabilities through conduct training. Structuring the meetings and sticking to the defined roles and responsibilities help create a safe environment where feelings, thoughts and fantasies are shared – as long as you stick to the structure. Finally, it is important to conduct regular assessments of the board that include an appraisal of board dynamics. In recruiting new members, your board should look at both the required hard skills as well as diversity, on the personal level.

In your own role, you can always keep trying to work on balancing both the goal-rational field and the psychodynamic field and work with the regression area. If you do not meet with understanding and openness towards solving the Gordian knot that is board dynamics, you should decide for yourself if this board can fulfill its role and responsibilities.

Remember, you are responsible for all decisions made by the board and, despite your comments and remarks in the minutes, if the company fails, you are financially liable. Even if you have insurance, the lawyers can still drag you through a long process to investigate whether you intentionally made fatal decisions.

Chapter 6
Talent-Based Board Work
by Leo Smith

Author's note: Let me introduce Leo Smith, the contributing writer and author of this chapter. Leo has served on the book's board, and we collaborated closely in developing this work. Our talents complement each other, and through mutual respect, we have transformed them into valuable assets for this book's creation. I hope you enjoy his insights in this chapter.

This chapter could also be called "Me on the Board." Why is that? Going back to the notion of agency developed in Chapter 2, the simplest answer is, because you matter. Your unique perspectives, knowledge and skills as well as your blind spots and drawbacks can have a tremendous impact on the success or failure of the organization. Therefore, in this chapter, we will zoom in on you and your role when you bring the best possible version of yourself to the boardroom. Why is this important? Your unique contributions are part of what makes the board a diverse place. The operational organization needs your special talents to be able to keep up with the increasing complexity they are facing and will continue to face in the future.

But it's not as simple as it sounds. We will also look at what can go wrong when you show up as your best possible self. Your particular aptitudes are a double-edged sword, and handling them takes constant, mindful practice.

In this chapter, you will learn about the concept of "requisite variety," which will help you understand the importance of talent diversity and inclusivity on the board. We will also take a more nuanced look at what it means to do strategy, as well as how to couple talents with the two other main board activities, governance and setting the C-level.

We will look at how you can leverage your unique talents in the boardroom and invite others to do the same. The idea of talent (or strengths) can be used to create both self-awareness and insight about other members. It helps you build a shared and inclusive vocabulary so that everyone can have a voice in the boardroom.

And when things go wrong, there are a few useful methods for getting things back on track. Specifically, you will see that an appreciation of other people's differences and some self-reflection can go a long way.

PERSPECTIVE

The Importance of Understanding Talents

The world is changing faster than ever. Technological developments, new rising economies and political tensions are just a few of the things that influence organizations today. But what does this have to do with you in a board setting?

When you're dealing with a complex environment, the operational organization and especially the board of directors need to have a matching level of diversity. This means that the organization relies on the diverse knowledge and perspectives of all board members when making large-scale, long-term decisions. So, the future success of the organization is partly dependent on you bringing your unique point of view, know-how and talents to the table. You also have to recognize your own biases, blind spots and weaknesses, as well as your capacity to bring out the strengths of both the board members and the C-level executives. In short, it is your duty to bring your best possible self (or selves) to the board room and to facilitate the same in others. It also is your job to keep developing and honing your talents and skills and encourage other members to do the same.

To illustrate this, we will look at an example from a board which will be referred to throughout the chapter. The company is a scale-up tech company. The current board was recently established to help take the company to the next level while ensuring that investors also got their money's worth. To start a more strength-based collaboration on the board, we did a joint session in which the team's strengths and blindspots were laid out based on psychometric testing. It turned out that they had a strong tendency towards speed, momentum and general risk aversion. While these trends are very useful in a start-up setting, they may not help with scaling profitably and governance demands. The group also showed a potential for long-term planning and overview, but a possible weak spot in terms of understanding people, which could be an issue when hiring the C-team.

That being said, each board member brought unique strengths to the table that could offset the weaknesses. We then started working on specific practices that could help bring the unique talents to the table.

For instance, one team member was highly detail-oriented and data-driven, which allowed her to be skeptical. However, she also was a bit of a dreamer. To overcome this, the team agreed to have a formal phase in all major decision-making processes where she was specifically asked to be the devil's advocate. That way, they created a space for her skepticism to shine and the others were "forced" to listen and adapt to her input.

But before moving on, what does "talent" really mean? While there are many ways of defining talent, the definition I use in this chapter comes from Clifton and Harter who defined talent as "our naturally recurring patterns of thought, feeling and behavior that can be productively applied."[48] Talents are not the same as competencies, knowledge and skills. All those things can be taught. For example, you can learn how to use Excel to do basic quantitative analyses. You can learn the legal basics of good governance. You can learn how to structure board meetings in terms of content, preparation and so on. But talents cannot be taught. They are your preferred way of seeing, sensing, thinking about and acting in the world.

This does not mean that talents equal performance! What it means is that your talents are the foundation for your development as a board member. You need to develop them, reflect on them and fine-tune them in the context of the board room. Referring to the example from before, the skeptical-yet-dreamy board member must use, fine-tune and evaluate both her skeptical and visionary dreamer talents as they come into play.

Pay Attention When Working With Talents

While having diverse minds is key to building responsive and strategically relevant boards, diversity is nothing without inclusion. To be able to access the board's talents, everyone has to feel free to voice their opinion and bring their talents to the table.

It is not easy getting the right mix of talents and skills on the board. On top of that, creating a space where everyone feels heard and where different perspectives can flourish productively is even harder. One of the culprits lies in the talents themselves. In our boardroom example, the speed-oriented talents had overwhelmed and silenced the skepticism on the team.

So, while your talents may be your biggest assets, they may also hold you back. This happens when your top talents overly dominate your worldview. For example, if you are particularly strong in analytical thinking and data analysis, you may think emotions and feelings are irrelevant. Essentially, your talents can become prejudices that prevent you from acknowledging other ways of thinking, feeling and behaving. That's to say, they could make you biased. Moreover, a high-pressure environment tends to bring out your most dominant talents.

So, what should you be aware of, in yourself? A good rule of thumb is that, whenever you find someone to be extremely annoying and incapable of just "getting it," remember that part of the problem is on your side, too. Also, consider that the annoying aspect of the other person's behavior is probably the result of a talent. So, it could be a potentially useful asset, even if it's currently not being fully expressed.

Finally, keep in mind that not having any differences of opinion on the board is a threat as well. You need to have disagreeing and challenging perspectives. If everyone always agrees, it means you probably lack a diversity mindset. What matters is how you handle differing viewpoints. In our example from before, the board managed to build a structure to support the skeptical voice. However, it takes considerable, collective practice to make sure that critical viewpoints are actually considered.

What You Need to Know

Practically all organizations are becoming more complex. All kinds of societal, environmental, legal and political forces are putting intense pressure on organizations, requiring them to be ever more adaptive. It is probably safe to say that the good old days of five-year prescriptive strategies are gone. But what then? Should we just give in to the chaos and give up planning entirely? Moreover, how can you, as an individual board member, leverage your talents to become a valuable strategy resource for the company in the future?

Complexity and Emergent Strategizing

It is broadly accepted that complexity is unavoidable for all organizations, now and in the future. But before focusing on what you can do about it, let's take a step back and look at a very fundamental question: How do organizations cope with complexity?

The term "complex" is often used interchangeably with "complicated" but they are very different. A complicated situation is one where outcomes are predictable. It may be difficult and require some complicated modeling, but at the end of the day, you pretty much know what to expect. Complex, however, refers to a situation where the same starting point can lead to different outcomes depending on how variables interact with each other. And some of these may be completely unknown. As an example, building a business intelligence system is complicated (predictable), but the implementation of a business intelligence system is complex because it involves people interacting in various unpredictable ways with the system and each other.

As a board member, knowing the difference is crucial. It allows you to apply the right type of logic to the issue. As you will see below, knowing which talents you tend to use by default is a valuable insight because it makes you aware of your own biases and blind spots.

Below, I explain two concepts that you can use as a foundation for how to bring your best possible self to the table. Both concepts address how to handle complexity in board work: Emergent strategizing and ensuring requisite variety.

Emergent Strategizing

Emergent strategizing is a fresh new look at what strategy is. In the past, strategy was thought of as the output of a rational-logical analysis.

The original definition of strategy emphasized long-term goals and objectives. It focused on action plans and allocating resources to achieve these goals.[49]

The main concern in classic strategy was always, "What is the strategy?" This perspective makes a few key assumptions:

- **Predictability.** The world is assumed to be predictable, otherwise, a three- to five-year plan would be meaningless.

- **Rationality of strategic actors.** Strategic actors are the executives and the board. The assumption is that they are capable of objectively laying out all the right facts and rationally choosing between many options to eventually pick the best one.

- **Unequivocal causality.** Tying back to the points above, they assume that they objectively know beforehand both the causes and outcomes of their decisions and actions.

There are many examples of classic strategizing gone wrong as a result of the faulty assumption of predictability. One popular example, covered by both *Forbes* and the *Economist*, involved a renowned management consulting firm and a telecom giant. In the 1980s, telco giant AT&T asked McKinsey about the future potential of the market for cellular phones. The consultants concluded that by the year 2000, the total market would be around 900,000 subscribers. The actual number of cellphone users in 2000 was closer to 109 million.

While these assumptions of classic strategy may still be true in some organizations that you know of, they are probably not valid for most companies in the current business market. AI and quantum computing are now gaining serious momentum. And while the COVID shutdown was hardly part of strategy decision-making at the time, such an event can certainly have a tremendous impact on how businesses operate.

Emergent strategizing gives you a different way of looking at strategy. While most of the classic strategy researchers had an academic background in economy and math, researchers from the emergent camp were trained in sociology, anthropology and the general arts. So, the old school leaned toward quantitative analyses and mathematical modeling, whereas the new school used an approach based on cultural observations of what actually happened in strategy work.

Classical strategizing gave us the strategy tools that you most likely already know from textbooks, such as Porter's Value Chain, the 5 Forces and Ansoff's Growth Matrix. These tools include the "What" of strategy by guiding our conversations. The emergent perspective gives insights into the intricacies of the strategizing process. As it turns out, actual strategy work is not as linear as you would think. And, not surprisingly, strategy actors are not super-rational decision-makers either. The emergent perspective helps us understand the "How" of strategizing. Your job as a board member is to appreciate both methods by mindfully using your unique talents and skills.

According to Mintzberg, strategy is best described as patterns in a series of decisions.[50] These patterns may happen on purpose or not. But in practically all cases, strategy involves both intentional and unintentional patterns. A rather stark example of this is Eleiko, the world's leading producer of weightlifting equipment, barbells and plates. The company started out making waffle irons, and their transition into weightlifting equipment was not a deliberate strategic decision. As the story goes, the factory supervisor was an avid weightlifter who got fed up with the poor quality of available equipment and persuaded the managing director to produce a few barbells and some plates to use with it. Six years later in 1963, the bar was introduced to the world during the World Championships in Stockholm and things really took off.

The basic idea, from the emergent perspective, is to work with strategy as a process. So rather than laying out a definite plan, building an emergent strategy is a constant balance between observing, testing and adjusting. I am not saying that planning is useless, but using an emergent approach means being more experimental and adaptive.

To get a deeper understanding of strategizing, let us look at the three P's:[51]

- **Practices.** These are any kind of routine or behavior, tools and methods used in making the strategy, such as strategy away-days, or the power of PowerPoint presentations and agendas.

- **Practitioners.** These are the roles, identities and identity dynamics of all strategic actors involved. Strategic actors are not only board members and chief executives, but could also be consultants.

- **Praxis.** This is the concrete strategy making, at the micro-level. What is being said and done by whom, when, how and with what effect?

When you take into account the three P's of strategizing, you open your mind to thinking critically about how you and your board work together.

To make better decisions, you need to optimize how you cooperate to make sure that you are getting the most out of the board's human capital. The decisions you make collectively are rooted in this collaboration.

The example referred to at the beginning of the chapter showed how one particular board member (a Practitioner) had something valuable to add to the board, and how the board facilitated this by creating a specific Practice around her playing the "devil's advocate."

So, what should you, as a new board member, retain from this? First, that strategy is more than just "the strategy." This is not to say that forming a plan and the corresponding courses of action is not important. But in an increasingly complex world, you also have to consider the process of strategy work. You must focus not only on which decisions are made, but also how decisions are made. You can pay attention to how certain practices encourage or hold back some ideas and how things could be thought of differently. When you do that, you start building a board whose way of working can handle complexity.

For you, as an individual board member, it is important to understand that you are part of the process. Your actions or lack of them not only influence decision making, but even more, how decisions are made. Start thinking about how certain practices facilitate certain series of decisions while other practices blind you. Also, think about how practices and psychodynamics encourage or silence certain voices. What can you do to make sure everyone is heard? For instance, if a company wants to be customer-centric, how can you ensure that the actual voice of the customer is considered during strategizing?

Reshaping how you think about strategy is an important step in constructing strong boards and building your capacity as a board member. But it is not enough. You also need to understand how every single board member brings something different to the table. That is, how do board members' individual differences create variety?

Requisite Variety and Talent

How do systems, such as organizations, cope with their environment? According to Ashby, when there is more variety in the surrounding environment than the internal variety of a system, the environment eventually destroys the system.[52] So, an organization that is not as diverse as its environment will die. Therefore, as the diversity of the environment around most organizations increases, the more you need strategic decision-makers with a variety of perspectives.

In the board mentioned earlier, there was actually quite a bit of talent diversity, even though the entrepreneurial spirit had a tendency to take over. In addition to the skeptical member, the board also had a member who was highly enthusiastic about coaching and mentoring members of the C-suite. Another rather quiet member was a strong diplomat. So, discussions were much more productive when all the different voices had a say.

As a member of the board, your role is to bring variety to the system so that the organization can survive in an increasingly complex world. So how do you do that? The short answer: You bring all of your talents and skills with you. You must recognize both your unique strengths and your particular biases and blind spots. You also need to pay attention to and encourage the strengths that other board members bring to the mix. Sounds simple, right? Unfortunately, it is not so easy. But if you make a habit of paying attention to these things, you can. Let us take a look at how you can do that.

Cognitive Diversity and Talent

Boards are a resource for strategic planning and decision-making. Research has shown that having a cognitively diverse board is essential to their ability to do strategic problem-solving. Cognitive diversity is defined as a difference in perspective or way of processing information.[53]

If you look at an organization as a complex system that has to adapt to very dynamic and unpredictable environments, cognitive diversity in boards is arguably more important than ever. Therefore, boards need a variety of skills, competencies, knowledge and talent.

In this chapter, I will focus more on talents than skills, knowledge and competence. Think of the latter factors as basic requirements to first get a seat at the table. Talents are part of what sets you apart and allows you to make unique contributions.

Using your talents to bring value to board strategizing clearly involves other people, such as other board members and C-level executives. So let us look at a very simple model for using talent in social settings. As a board member, the model explained in the next section can help you understand not only your own talents but also how they relate to and interact with the talents of your fellow board members.

Talents in Complex Adaptive Systems: Supplementary and Complementary Fit

Person-Organization theory[54] gives a good base for understanding how your talents can be used and developed on the board. This is because Person-Organization fit is a good predictor of performance. In this section, we will look at a way of working with your talents based on this theory.

First of all, what do I mean by "fit"? And fit in "where"? To keep things simple, we can look at fit from two different angles: person-task fit and person-group fit.

A cautionary note before we continue: It is easy to misunderstand fit as something static or a fixed state. However, fit is not static at all. Think of it as continuous fitting, that is, as a verb. It is the continued fitting that allows the board to cope with increasing complexity.

In addition to strategy, the primary task of the board is to protect shareholder interests by ensuring a running business that is compliant with proper governance and risk management and to hire (or at least approve) members of the C-suite. Your unique combination of talents will probably match up differently with these tasks of board work.

There is no such thing as the perfect board-member fit. It is, quite simply, not possible to excel in all aspects of board work. The best you can do is think about which of your strengths to bring into play. When the topic at hand gets your top talents fired up, it is time to step up and use your talents to the fullest. Also, recognize that some topics are just not your home turf. In this case, you may want to consider how you can participate in this process, again bringing your strengths to the table, while recognizing you are accountable for all decisions made by the board.

With person-group fit, there is a certain subtlety to consider. You could argue that fit means that the talents of a person should overlap with those of the group. Or you could say that a good fit fills in the gaps, like pieces in a jigsaw puzzle. Overlapping talents are usually called supplementary fit whereas filling in the gaps is complementary fit. So which should you focus on?

Actually, both types of fit are valuable and can co-exist.[55] Indeed, having a shared foundation from which individual differences can be brought into play is how a board can cope with complexity (via differences) while maintaining a sense of stability. Ideally, board members share core organizational values and goals while also showing up with their unique talents. In this way, they use the diversity in the team.

It is important to keep in mind that fit is not static. It is a continuous process and requires the constant effort of everyone involved. A board might be a good fit on paper, but if they do not commit to the process of fitting, it's no use. Returning to our case, the board aligned on the importance of speed and agility but, going into a scaling phase, they needed to expand on this to ensure efficiency. So, while tempo was still important, the board needed to add more structured follow-ups on metrics about operational performance. Having this as a strategic priority was also part of ensuring proper governance, so they needed to hire a CCO. Previously these responsibilities sat with the CEO, but it was never a great fit with his talents. Carving out the operational responsibilities allowed the CEO to do more of what he did best, which was doing brand ambassadorship with all key stakeholders.

But how do you work with complementary and supplementary fit within the board? Practically speaking, there is a two-step process for achieving this. First, the board, as a group, needs to plainly state their common values and goals – the basic principles according to which work is done and the general direction the organization is going in. Once this is laid out, each board member can demonstrate how their top talents contribute to the group. Having a shared core and many voices and perspectives when making decisions makes the board better able to handle their own complexity and that of the environment. For you, this means being aware of your specific talents and being able to talk about them clearly. The practical way to do this will be addressed below.

Secondly, look at what fit really means for the board members' most important interactions. A member has to understand how their talents can be brought into play with the three stakeholder groups: the board as a team, the executive team, and the shareholders/stakeholders that they represent. These groups are dynamic and are influenced by you. But these groups also bring out certain aspects of your talents. This group-interaction dynamic is important because it's important to avoid uniformity and homogeneity on the board. If the board or executive team tends to be optimistic and bold thinking, play the devil's advocate and challenge this optimism. If they are conservative and change-averse, then challenge that.

These stakeholder groups are made up of different kinds of people, each with their own unique strengths and weaknesses. So, it is valuable to consider each individual as well. Think again about which talents you align with and which you don't. It's the differences, in particular, that you can leverage to access each other's strengths. For instance, imagine that you and the CEO align on being analytical and data-driven, but you are more empathic than he or she is. So, you can contribute by finding common ground on a strategic decision with numbers and facts that also take into account the emotional impact of the decision. Bringing both perspectives to the table allows for a better decision. On the one hand, this is how cognitive diversity gives a strategic edge. But on the other, it may make you want to throw the other person out the window!

What You Need to Do

Talents are assessed differently than skills, knowledge and competencies. You can test the latter with an exam. For example, it is not difficult to find out whether someone has the necessary legal knowledge to join the board. Talents, on the other hand, require special testing methods.

There are many tools available, such as Gallup's CliftonStrengths, VIA Institute's Character Strengths, Talents Unlimited's TT38 and Alex Linley's Strength profile. While there are differences between them, they all share a foundation in positive/strength psychology and help you discover your unique talents and weaknesses. What's more, they give you a precise vocabulary to use when discussing your strengths and weaknesses. What is important to remember, however, is that all useful talent and strengths assessments show a range of potentials as well as their drawbacks. In short, everyone brings many different talents to the table. For instance, you may be analytical and facts-oriented while also being generally optimistic about things. In this case, your task is to work on improving both these talents and make sure that they are brought into play at the right moment. Your own internal variety of talents can give you insights into how you can develop as a board member. One development trajectory could be how to control and confine the drawbacks of your particular talent. For instance, being risk-oriented is great, but not if your default answer to everything is a plain "no."

Referring back to the case of the appointed devil's advocate, the skeptic board member will have to keep practicing how to deploy her talents. This involves reflections on how her skepticism is voiced, when to voice it, to whom and under which circumstances. She also has to know when not to be skeptical.

It is essential that you practice so you can develop your individual talents. Being on a board should never be your final destination. It should be part of a journey that allows you to grow and add even more value to the organization.

To summarize, do a talent and strength assessment to find out what your unique contributions are and how you can develop them. To make them more meaningful for others (and yourself), find some examples of how and when your talents have flourished and the positive outcomes that resulted from them.

A Talent Toolbox Analogy

Essentially, you can look at your talents as an incomplete toolbox. You may have a hammer, a screwdriver and a wrench, but lack a tape measure and pliers. The point here is that no one is a complete board member, nor will they ever be. Ideally, everyone brings their different tools to the problem at hand and carefully decides how to use them. But just because you have these tools, it doesn't mean that you are naturally good at using them for specific tasks. You have to practice. For instance, by studying and trying them out with others. At the end of the day, they have to be used and reflected upon afterward.

Specific tasks and contexts may require different tools from your box. But everyone tends to reach for the same tool, regardless of the situation. One key to personal talent development as a board member is to use all the tools in your toolbox.

Unfortunately, the toolbox analogy has its limits. It may be easy to add new tools to a real toolbox, but it is a lot harder to add talents. Instead of trying to add more talents, why not acknowledge that you are an incomplete human being? Recognizing your weaknesses is important. But keep in mind that it is no excuse to underperform. Ideally, you can find someone on the board with the talents you are missing and either delegate or get help. In some cases though, it is just a matter of sticking it out and doing what is needed.

In summary, here is what you can do to show up with your unique talents and contribute your voice to ensure a variety of perspectives on the board:

- Get a firm grasp of what your unique contributions are. How do you add to the diversity on the board?

- Explore your full range of talents.

- Consider how your talents contribute to the primary task of the board.

- In the context above, think about which talent domains you would like to develop.

- Explore when, how and with whom you express your various talents in the best possible way.

- Think critically about how your talents could also include prejudices and blind spots.

How to Practice

Before the first board meeting, understand your own strengths and weaknesses.

Your strengths are a valuable asset to making sure there is a requisite variety on the board. This first exercise is about understanding yourself and developing a nuanced vocabulary to describe exactly what you bring to the table.

First, choose a suitable talent test from those mentioned earlier in the chapter. Ideally, do a feedback session with a certified consultant so you can get some deeper insights (as some of these reports can be very comprehensive and difficult to read). Once you have your results, do the following:

- Write down six to seven aspects of your top talents that you can contribute to your board. These facets may seem opposing. For instance, you may be both optimistic but also quite skeptical. This allows you to have a dual outlook.

- Find one or two examples of what these talents look like by using a story. For instance, if you are particularly strong with knowledge deep-dives into specific topics, find a story that illustrates how this strength has been useful in the past

- Find out what your most likely blind spots are. These are

typically the drawbacks of your top talents. For example, if you are particularly strong in keeping a strategic overview of things, there is a risk of the low-hanging fruit fallacy. You will likely find yourself thinking "How difficult can it be?" when in reality, it might actually be quite difficult.

After each board meeting, reflect on how you played your talents.

To make sure that you show up with all your relevant possible selves and to ensure that the positive version of your talents is expressed, do a short reflection on how your talents played out during a meeting. A short five-minute reflection using the following questions will take you a long way:

- How did you put your talents to good use in the meeting? Find three examples.

- How did your top talents play out in a less-than-optimal way in the meeting? Find at least one example.

- What were the circumstances that drove the examples above? Think of context, topics and your own emotions, as well as other board members and their behaviors.

Going forward, which specific talent domains do you want to practice to continuously improve your contributions to the board?

Your journey as a board member is a continuous development process. Once you have laid out your talents and participated in a few board meetings, you should start mapping out a personal development trajectory, using the following core questions:

- Which aspect(s) of your talents do you want to specifically develop over the course of the next year?

- What does progress in these domains look like?

- Where can you find resources to help you leverage your strengths? This may be in the form of knowledge pursuits (courses, books, podcasts and so on), mentoring (who does this really well and how can you pick their brains?) and seeking active feedback from other board members and executives.

How to Recover

Acknowledging that you and your talents could create conflict or cause collaboration to fail is the first step to coming back. While it's hard to admit it, it is also a powerful realization because it means that you can influence it for the better. Therefore, think back and reflect on which of your talents might have been in overdrive and the context and interactive situation that provoked it. Then, try to figure out which of the other person's talents clashed with yours.

For example, if the other board member is extremely detail-oriented and you are not, this may be part of the frustration. Also, identify where you have overlapping talents. Maybe both of you are very goal-oriented.

Now that you have done that, arrange a conversation with the person that is annoying you. Structure the meeting by first pointing out that you feel that the collaboration is not optimized and that you want to find a way to use each other's differences in the best way possible.

Then, you can identify together which overlapping talents you have. This helps form some common ground.

Next, you can both look at your differing talents and express to each other how his or her talent is particularly special, ideally using a concrete example. Having done this, you can now center your conversation around when and how your different talents can be a valuable asset but also how and when they are the source of frustration.

Finally, remember that some people, unfortunately, are incapable of self-reflection and will stick to the same annoying pattern for the rest of their lives. In these cases, it is time to ask yourself whether working on that particular board is worth it to you.

Chapter 7

How to Understand Dynamics in Board Committees

In the introduction of this book, we touched upon how today's boards are overloaded with information. More and more professional subjects end up on the board's table as the world develops, expands and goes through crises. Therefore, we need even more committees to address these topics.

Committees are subgroups of the board consisting of both selected board members and employees from the operational organization. Their primary task is to prepare and present specific areas to the full board for resolution in the board.

Over the last decade, many boards have added committees or expanded existing ones to accommodate new areas such as sustainability and technology; the latter includes digital transformation and cybersecurity. In the present day, committees are aligning with the strategic focus of the board and shifting towards governance priorities. They now have to take into account broader stakeholder interests – all this while adapting to the challenges their operational organizations come up against. This change in the structure of the goal-rational field adds to the complexity of the board dynamics. It opens the door for new ways of working with and in the committees.

Up until recently, the board has generally consisted of the board members and a group that prepares board materials. This included the chairperson, the vice chair, the CEO and the deputy CEO or CFO. In some countries, governance regulations require listed companies to have the following committees: audit and risk, remuneration and nomination. The last may be part of the remuneration committee. Other committees can be, for example, strategy, technology, ESG, and many more based on the type of organization the board oversees.

Being conscious of the special position of a committee and its role (what to do and not to do) is a new area to explore. It requires exactly the same attention to the dynamics as is given to the operational organization and the board, as described in the previous chapters. When looking at committees, you also need to analyze the board and how your talents play out.

You have already been introduced to what makes boards different from regular operational organizations. In this chapter, you will get insights into how committees differ from both regular operational organizations and the board as an organization. Furthermore, we look at how the committees affect the dynamics of the board. This is because when the board creates more committees, it also allows for interaction with the operational organization and as such, crosses boundaries.

In committee work, you can apply everything you have already learned in this book. In addition, you will also be introduced to another way of supporting and facilitating committees to be as efficient and value-creating as possible, all the while avoiding the chances of them making decisions belonging to the board or the operational organization, or that they close in on themselves.

ᷣᷣ The Importance of Creating Value in Committees

Understanding how to create value in a committee is crucial because it enhances the effectiveness and efficiency of the decision-making processes within a board. In this way, committees can reduce the workload for boards that have to address the rapid changes in the world. Committees allow the board to delegate specialized tasks related to the strategy. This requires leveraging the expertise of committee members and consequently, requires creating a space for learning.

Committees provide a platform for diverse perspectives, innovation and thorough problem-solving. Effective committee work includes accountability and clear communication, which are necessary as the board does not delegate the decision-making to the committees.[56]

To illustrate the important work of committees, let us look at an example of a customer committee in a Danish utility company (water, heating etc). The goal of this committee was to listen to and get closer to the customers. The committee consisted of two board members who were elected by customers every four years, and of one or more employees, depending on what was on the agenda. The role of the committee was to take up strategic subjects related to the customer. This was done by establishing a so-called Customer Forum comprising 20 to 30 customers appointed in such a way that different customer types are represented. The Customer Forum serves an advisory function to the board and every meeting starts with members stating the purpose of the group, which was, "The customer forum has a voice and the board decides."

When you look at this customer committee and the forum, you can see that the committee "chews" the information to aid the board's decision-making. Additionally, the committee communicates to the forum what the board has decided.

In order for the customer committee to fulfill its task, it is necessary to understand that the committee operates on the boundary between the board and the operational organization. Both board members and employees cross boundaries, so you must be conscious of this. Crossing boundaries creates a space for innovation because it allows for diverse perspectives to be heard and for collaboration across different areas of expertise. It requires creativity and a willingness to communicate and integrate different ideas.

In the case of the Danish utility company, learning took place in different ways, both in the committee and in the Customer Forum: through presentations of technical information, listening to both the customers' experience and their expertise or listening to the experts in the operational organization. In addition, the board members also had their own particular expertise to present.

Since learning is a key factor in committees, we need to be conscious of creating this learning space so that the committee can create value.

In any group you enter, the dynamics come into play. Above the surface, we can see that when there is a change in board structure and more committees are added, board members and employees connect more often. Previously, board members collectively met employees only at board meetings. With more committees present, the board members and employees will meet more often and at a random frequency.

These changes influence the goal-rationality area of the boardroom dynamics because some members have more information about the operational organization than others. It affects the psychodynamic field as well since relationships form and conscious and unconscious groups and boundaries may appear. Roles may change. There may be a promotion of some committees as opposed to others. For example, the audit and risk committee could become more important than the social media committee. Their statuses are probably prioritized according to which topic aligns more closely with the core business of the company and the primary task of the board. Moreover, you would probably need additional talents for your committee work as opposed to those needed for your work on the board.

You can use all the knowledge from previous chapters and apply it to committees so that you can show up with competency and confidence. However, the environment in a committee requires, as mentioned above, a vital focus on the creation of a sound learning space. This is because it allows committees to better create value for the board and the organization.

Be aware that you may find various theories on learning that cannot be applied fully to committees. It is not the optimal way of working since a board committee cannot truly implement a learning community. So, this chapter will introduce what could be done to implement a supportive learning space in committee work.

Pay Attention When Analyzing Committee Dynamics

Changing the board structure to include more committees is a way of dealing with the increasing need for expertise in the boardroom. It is also a way of providing company-specific knowledge for the board. Quite often, it is difficult or even impossible to bring all board members up to the same knowledge level. Working through committees is a productive way to link the specifics of the company to the work on the board.

Creating more committees requires more management and communication. In my experience, these two areas tend to break down. In one case, the first time the committee members met with the operational organization, they asked for information – interrogation-style. As a result of this lack of communication about the committee's intention, they never met with the operational organization again.

If committees do not have clear points of reference, expectations and a common understanding, the group is likely to stop working. They could even fall into the stages of basic assumption as described in Chapter 5.

Another issue that could arise is that the committee may become too settled. By this, I mean that they forget that their goal is only to process the material and present it to the board for decision-making. Some committees, particularly risk and audit committees, tend to be deeply involved and know so many details that the presentation of accounts to the board becomes a formality. It may be nice to have someone on the board picking up this task, but in the end, it is all board members who are responsible. When committees present materials that are too well prepared, board members may fear asking "stupid" questions and as such, be at risk of blinding themselves.

Apart from the risk of the committee becoming too insular, at the other end of the spectrum, there are also risks associated with turning committees into learning spaces. A learning space requires a more informal and self-structured environment, which may create anxiety in the committee members. Structure is often a way to create safety. In the Tavistock experiential learning, a firm frame is a way to create a safe place for playful creativity.

Committees work on the boundary between the board and the operational organization. So, one other risk is that the board becomes too involved in operational work. For example, when the audit and risk committee prepares the Annual Financial Report, the board members can become so deeply involved that they become part of making the Financial Report. If this work becomes too deep, the board members on the committee may end up supervising their own work.

When you engage your talents, you always run the risk of showing up too strong with one talent or forgetting to tone down another one which is not adequate for the task at hand. For example, if one of your top talents is being highly critical (the assessing talent), then you should keep your criticism to yourself by writing it down whenever the committee is working on new ideas or is in a learning process. To support people with this talent, the committee should structure the meeting with two dedicated breaks where criticism is the sole topic. This could be a way to support both learning and criticism.

While in the learning zone, you may discover that not everyone can adapt to this way of working. It may seem too soft or too unstructured. Welcoming all input and uncertainty can create a chaotic space which some people may find difficult and unnecessary.

Moreover, adding the learning dimension to the committee may create a conflict between performance (for example, a product must be developed for the board within a certain time frame) and learning (committee members need to learn so that they can freely create a valuable product). This could also cause a struggle between the established organizational structure and the learning agenda.

For example, if the customer committee only focuses on creating a learning environment, the committee may not get to the point of creating a specific agenda for the Customer Forum. As such the customer committee does not comply with the charter given by the board.

All in all, you will find that working in committees is both effective and challenging. The committees do have various possibilities for conflicts since they operate on the boundary between the board and the operational organization. These challenges are seen when analyzing above and below the surface, when applying your talents to committee work and especially when creating the learning space in the committee.

What You Need to Know

Working with and in committees requires you to be conscious. You have to use the psychodynamic organizational systems framework and the talents framework. To top it all off, you should understand and ideally implement a learning space or, at least, a learning mindset.

In Chapters 3, 4 and 5, you learned how to analyze the board. In the previous chapter, you saw how to bring your talents into play and even more importantly, which to employ and when. This section goes deeper into a new area of exploration, the learning space, where you will be introduced to what learning in committees implies.

The Difference Between a Committee and a "Pure" Learning Space

Before getting into the subject of learning, you must be aware of the difference between a committee and a "pure" learning space, meaning an environment meant solely for learning.

Committee work requires more structure than a space developed for the sole purpose of learning. Often, the chairperson of the committee is the board member who possesses the particular expertise needed. For example, the chairperson of the risk and audit committee is often the board member with the most knowledge and experience in the financial domain. With respect to providing the material for the committee, the facilitators are often senior management. For example, the CEO is the facilitator of the strategy committee.

It is the responsibility of the committee chair to run the meeting and of executive management to drive the learning process. For instance, a board may dedicate one hour before the formal board meeting for the executive management to run a deep dive into a specific topic for all the members. For some boards, these deep dives are prepared by the committee that has this topic as its primary task.

In the learning space, a facilitator is the person who guides the processes, encourages participation and creates a collaborative environment. This needs to be included in the description of the role of the committee chairperson so that another leader does not take on the job.[57]

Your committee will most likely be a group of four to 10 people. As a learning space, it often brings together many people in the same domain and with similar roles, but from different organizations. This provides more ways to facilitate learning in smaller subgroups and the like. So, by inviting a learning space into the committee, you are essentially providing an environment where people listen, are open to insecurity and are willing to learn from each other.

In short, a pure learning space is collaborative, often including peers within a community. Conversely, a committee is also a part of an organizational structure with specific organizational issues. Unlike a "pure" learning space, a committee has a specific task to carry out and must return to the board with a product. The committee is, as previously mentioned, a place for leveraging knowledge on the board and as such a space where learning happens and should be considered in the work of the members.

A Light Model of Learning in a Committee

Committees are different from pure learning spaces, but they can benefit from creating an environment with elements of learning.

Below, you will be introduced to how this could look and how you can support such a learning space as a member of a committee.

How to Apply Learning to Board Committees

Any committee member can foster collaboration by encouraging open dialogue and knowledge sharing among members, which builds synergy. This can be achieved through regular meetings and workshops where members discuss and learn from each other. For example, in one committee, an expert was invited to provide their expertise to the group. Afterward, they were invited to the board meeting so that all members could also gain this knowledge.

Committee members should spotlight and legitimize self-awareness, self-management, social awareness, relationship skills and social responsibility in the "chewing" material process. By focusing on and training in these areas, you increase the chances of having good communication, empathy and teamwork.

The committee should develop a common language for discussing issues to ensure clarity and mutual understanding among members. This creates a safe learning space to understand where everyone is coming from.

Part of the charter of the committee should include regular assessments of how effective the committee work is. These assessments should include learning initiatives within the committee that identify areas for improvement while making sure they stay aligned with the strategic goals and charter of the board.[58]

Facilitator

Facilitators support reflection. This means that everyone has the opportunity to contribute because the facilitator maintains a neutral environment for developing the material for the board. They build trust, enhance social skills and promote independence among the committee members.

It is important to cultivate social relationships. This may be done using various group methods such as voicing dynamics in the group, setting the scene for learning physically (such as people sitting in a circle) and creating a secure environment for open communication and engagement. In the previous chapters, you saw that creating a safe space starts with trusting that you are entering a safe place when you come into the room.

You as a Member of the Committee

In Chapter 2, you saw how important it is to have agency within the board and in committees as well. You should explore your own agency, that of other members, as well as that of the group. This is not an easy task, but start by looking at your own sense of agency by monitoring yourself and your learning strategies. Ask questions out of curiosity. Engage in your own and other people's learning. If you see an openness to insecurity and to asking questions, you may be experiencing agency in the group.

A good learning environment is a place where people feel comfortable engaging and being the first mover on the elements mentioned above (self-awareness, self-management, social awareness etc). This is done by communicating openly and respectfully and sharing knowledge. Empathy, active listening and trust are important skills in learning spaces and building relationships. A couple of particularly important elements are genuine, respectful feedback and recognition of other members and the work done. Finally, you can use digital tools to share and leverage the knowledge of all members equally and support the common language. [59]

In the previously mentioned utility company example, there were two customer-elected board members. They ran a customer committee together with an executive assistant and experts in the operational organization. As we know, the committee was set up to "listen to the customers and provide better board knowledge from the customer area on strategy items." To listen, the committee elected 20 to 30 customers of various types (a customer forum). The election was done by choosing representatives of various customer types and other stakeholders. This is unlike other committees where the committee members are elected among the board and the employees. The members of the forum were approved by the board. They were informed that "the customer forum has a voice and the board decides." The forum was summoned one to three times a year to debate various subjects chosen by the customer committee, which were accepted by the board. The communication between the board and the customer forum went through the customer committee.

But how was this done, in reality? The above situation is a fine example of how a learning space was integrated into the rigid structure of a board and a committee.

The customer committee received instructions from the board on how to work with the customer forum. Then, the customer committee explored ideas on what to use the customer forum for, how to engage with it, how to leverage knowledge on a particular subject in the customer forum and how to listen actively and with curiosity.

All inputs were heard. If they were out of scope, the facilitators of the customer forum took note of items for future discussion.

Everything was recorded and brought to the board. One topic was the pricing of water and wastewater services. At the meeting, the customer group was introduced to how pricing restrictions work in the sector.

Afterwards, examples of projects were introduced. This included project costs, the outcome of the project and the price for the customer. It became clear to the participants that the cost of avoiding all overflows of wastewater would be exponentially higher than avoiding half of the overflows.

After the presentation, the customer forum split up into three groups and debates on three different subjects ran for 15 minutes. The results of these debates were presented in a plenum to get input from all types of customers. Everyone who wanted to add to the debate was free to speak. It was not the type of discussion where the forum needed to agree with each other since all input was relevant. From the forum, the customer committee brought the information back to the board so that they could understand the different pricing priorities of various customers. The whole forum meeting was facilitated by the board members in the customer committee.

The example above is special because learning took place in the customer forum, too. The space for learning was developed because it is a safe environment both in the committee and in the customer forum. Most members showed up with mutual respect and interest in participating. The work was managed to support this learning.

You may say it is just like any other group preparing a seminar. This is true. It is not a "pure" learning space. It is a learning environment implemented using a structured process. The most important thing to remember is that this work is done on the boundary between the board, the organization and the customers. This makes it challenging. However, a successful learning space can indeed be created.

Special Talents Needed in Committees

In the previous chapter, you were introduced to talents and how different ones are important in different settings. In a committee working on the boundaries of the board and the operational organization to process material and leverage knowledge, you will find that some talents are more in play than others. There will be some common talents for all types of committees and some that are specific to the committee and even for the business you are in.

Generally, a committee has three top priorities: The first would be to support collaboration, which points to talents such as team orientation, adaptability, conflict resolution and empathy.

The second is to learn, which points to talents such as curiosity, analytical thinking, self-reflection and persistence.

Finally, they need to communicate clearly, which points to talents such as active listening and clarity of expression.

An example of particular talents required in a specific committee could be the talent of analytic thinking and attention to detail. Analytical thinking is crucial for committees like audit or governance, where breaking down complex data and identifying patterns supports strategic decision-making and compliance oversight.

Attention to detail ensures precision in financial reviews, policy drafting and risk assessments, making it ideal for audit or finance committees where accuracy is critical.

What You Need to Do

Going back to the full view of a committee, the following exercises explain exactly what you can do to enhance value creation in your committees. They use both psychodynamic analysis with the organizational system view and psychodynamic elements, tapping into talent appreciation on the committee.

Finally, you can practice developing and supporting a learning space in your committees.

Understand Committees, Both Above and Below the Surface

- Know the committee charter laid down by the board, including the role of the chair, the purpose of the committee and the output required (the primary task).

- Explore the particular committee subject both internally and externally.

- Map the relationships and roles of the members – the whole above-the-surface system.

- Analyze the dynamics: roles, relationships and boundaries.

- Analyze your own internal dynamics.

- Map the perceived psychodynamic system, below the surface.

- Point out issues and address them.

Apply Talents to Committees

- Identify general talents needed in the committees.

- Find the specific talents necessary for this particular committee.

- Name the talents on the board and point out missing ones.

- Identify your own talents and figure out which to focus on and which to tone down.

Develop and Support the Learning Space

- Show trust.

- Monitor your own state of mind.

- Be curious about others.

- Make space for everyone, both the quiet and the noisy members.

- Show your own insecurities.

- Accept and support others in showing their insecurities.

How to Recover

In case a committee does not work properly, does not fulfill its responsibilities or does not create a respectful learning environment, you may have to work on many fronts.

First of all, the committee chair is responsible for ensuring that the committee performs according to the charter provided by the board. As such, the committee chair must go back to the committee in the following three areas: First, reintroduce the charter to the committee member; second, the committee chair must analyze the board below the surface and voice any issues; and third, the chair needs to look at the talents in play and check what is missing or which talents are blocking the work of the committee. The chair must express the positive points of all the talents and be a guide to show when certain talents should be active and when they should not be.

If the learning space is not fruitful, the chair should ensure that the learning space is recreated by showing up with his or her own agency, trust and respect. One method is to look at successful stories from outside the group or invite external advisors into a meeting to provide expertise.

As an individual member, you can support the chairperson of the committee by rejuvenating the right environment for the committee. In case it is stuck, you should go to the chairperson of the board to voice how the committee needs revitalization to kickstart performance in the committee.

Chapter 8

Quick Guide

This quick guide is intended to refresh your memory about what you have already read in this book. All of the most important points are summarized so that you can immediately apply them in your role as a board member. In addition, if there is any topic you would like to go back to and read in more detail, references are made to sections in each chapter.

Chapter 1 - The Framework: Above and Below the Surface of a Board

<u>Why</u>

Psychodynamic system theory gives you a framework to use while navigating the waters of board dynamics.

A board is a living organization. Like any other organization, it requires an understanding of leadership, followership and fellowship. The board has explicitly defined roles, tasks and boundaries, such as a chairperson or the primary task. However, there also exists soft roles, soft tasks and soft boundaries. These are either conscious or unconscious parts each person plays in the dynamics of the board, based on their emotional state, culture and life experiences. It is important to be aware of your soft roles, soft tasks and soft boundaries so you can decide which ones you want to play, which ones you do not want to play, and how to operate on the board.

Group dynamics is a subject that has been taken into account in the workplace for a long time. However, it is not so common in the boardroom. Bringing up such below-the-surface topics is sometimes not even taken seriously. But it is definitely worth the effort. Psychodynamic system theory can also help you understand situations where members wear more than one hat or when relationships between members change. Voicing these things makes board members consciously aware of what is going on under the surface. Being conscious of board dynamics can make all the difference in how successful a board is in achieving its goals.

In section 2 of Chapter 1, you will find many examples showing why it is so important to be aware of group dynamics in a board setting.

What

What Can Go Wrong

When you apply psychodynamics to the board room, you need to know the proper dosage – the when and how much of it. Being overly focused on the group dynamics can hinder progress just as much as not being conscious of it at all. In addition, being sensitive without being able to contain and mentalize, reflect on, and understand the feelings in yourself and in others can stall the work on the board.

If you don't pay any attention to the dynamics, you may miss how you and others influence the group. You may not understand your roles and responsibilities, which in the worst case, could jeopardize the primary task of the board and your reputation in the board world, and even result in financial liability.

Focusing too much on the below-the-surface dynamics can be equally risky. Exploring the interactions of the group takes time that boards may not always be willing to spend. You may just have to keep your observations to yourself, but they will still help you show up with confidence and competency.

Section 3 of Chapter 1 to read some cases of how things can go wrong when paying attention to board dynamics.

What You Need to Know

You are in an organization. This means you are in a group that shares a common primary task and its boundaries are clearly defined. You know why you are there and what you are there to do. You know who is in the group and who is not. You know your formal role and maybe even your informal roles, too. You receive input in the form of materials or skills from your members. You produce output, such as decisions or information for stakeholders.

The group dynamics framework used in this book is split into two fields: the goal-rational field and the psychodynamic field. The goal-rational field covers the explicitly stated roles, tasks and boundaries of the group. Part of the psychodynamic field is the unconscious zone, where people fill soft roles and express emotions, things that they are often not aware of. These two fields can influence each other, sometimes preventing one field from fulfilling its purpose. This is called regressive pressure.

For more details about each element of the framework, go to Chapter 1, section 4.

What You Need to Do

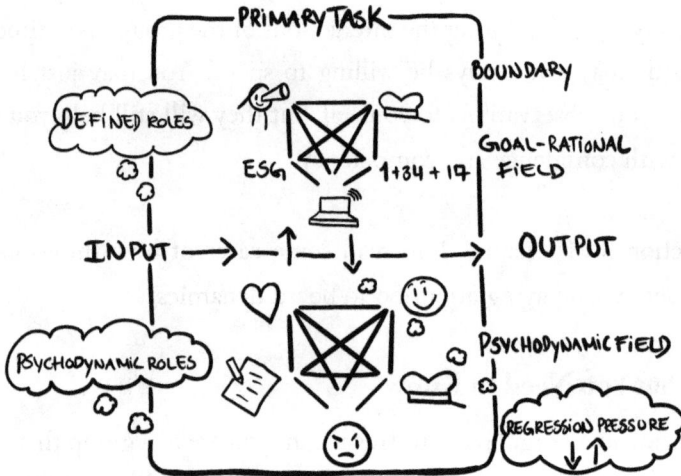

To better understand this framework, you need to examine several aspects of your board. Look at how the goal-rational field affects the dynamics of the group. Then look at what impact the psychodynamic field is having. You can then make a diagram of your organization like in the psychodynamic system model above. Attend a board meeting with the framework in mind and finally, reflect on your view of the board through this lens.

Go to section 5 of Chapter 1 to get a list of questions you can ask yourself to help you apply the model.

Chapter 2 - Agency and Boundaries: How to Be Confident in the Boardroom

<u>Why</u>

When you enter a board, you accept the responsibility of setting the course for the company. You are expected to exercise your rights as a board member. To do that with confidence and competency, you need to act with agency and be acutely aware of boundaries, be they yours, others' or the board's.

When you act with agency, you are aware of what you do and are accountable for it. When you have agency, others will be less likely to undermine it. A boundary is the line between what is part of the group and what is not. It is "a zone for connection, exchange, negotiation and transition," where boundaries both separate and connect – they remain semipermeable.

Personal boundaries are your own line showing where others may approach. Boundaries are there to protect you and the group. When you understand both formal and informal boundaries, you can better fulfill your role as a board member.

To better understand the nuances of agency and boundaries, go to Chapter 2, section 2.

<u>What</u>

What Can Go Wrong

Without agency and boundaries, the board cannot function properly. You may not be able to fulfill your role because you do not feel free to act accordingly. Or you may cross boundaries and end up taking on someone else's responsibilities.

There are also situations where you have one but not the other. For example, when you act with agency but do not respect boundaries, you may end up dominating the board when it may not be your role. This can cause confusion and a lack of direction. If the chair does not take steps to regain control, members may burn out or even resign. When you have boundaries, but no agency, work does not get done. The organizations on either side of the boundaries (for example, a committee and the board) are not able to communicate effectively and problems are not resolved.

For examples of breakdowns in agency and boundaries, go to Chapter 2, section 3.

What You Need to Know

At first glance, agency may seem like it applies only to how you act. But from a psychological point of view, agency has two parts: internal state and behavior. The internal state is about your relationship with yourself. When you feel that something isn't right, such as feeling like you are being taken advantage of, then you are tapping into the first part of agency. When you speak up about how you feel and clarify that the situation is not working for you, that is behavior and the second part of agency.

Clearly, agency drives behavior. Agency is the capacity to act, but it doesn't mean you can do whatever you want. You have to take into account the history and culture of the group you are entering and respect it. If you are a new member, for example, you may not feel agency until you learn about how the group functions.

But agency is not reserved only for people. Things can have agency as well. While objects may not have any free will, they can have a big impact on decision-making. Things like a legal document or a PowerPoint presentation could influence an important decision or guide a conversation. On an even more abstract level, an emotion is also a thing that can do things. These "things" have power, authority and agency because they represent human will, intentions and decisions, both in the goal-rational and psychodynamic fields. The point is, as a board member, you should be aware of anything that can have agency, be it human or not.

As you probably already know, a boundary is the line that sets the limit between two areas. In an organization, there is a conscious boundary that defines who is in the group or out. This important boundary helps keep you oriented. But there are also invisible boundaries that, when crossed, change the dynamics of the group. That doesn't mean that you should never cross boundaries. When you do, you should be well aware of it, communicate it clearly and have an exit plan to return to your previous place.

The formal system of an organization, such as a board, is outlined in the organizational chart. But there is also an informal system based on things members have in common. Sometimes, these shared characteristics fall under the umbrella of diversity. For the board to be able to benefit from this diversity, everyone's voice must be heard so that you can find compromises. To achieve the primary task of the board, you have to be conscious of both systems.

Boundaries are semipermeable and both separate and connect. Crossing boundaries can offer an opportunity for learning and creating value. Learning happens when you communicate across borders and return to your home base to reflect upon it. This way, you can gain new perspectives and discover new ideas, which leads to value creation.

While boundaries are necessary, they can also be a roadblock. Be aware and speak up when this occurs.

For examples and more details about agency and boundaries, see Chapter 2, section 4.

What You Need to Do

To apply what you have learned about agency, ask yourself questions about how you felt during the last board meeting. Think about what feelings you picked up from other members. Did you act consciously or were you reacting to something? Be sure to accept the agency of others, as well. Analyze how all elements, both human and non-human, contribute to the conversation. Make sure to take advantage of objects that can influence decision-making. Finally, practice some introspection to tap into your own agency.

Turning to boundaries, you can practice by first analyzing the ones on your board. You can facilitate learning and communicating across frontiers. Make sure that everyone gets to be heard. Pointing out differences actually helps find common ground. And if boundaries create a roadblock, say it. Also, look at how talent or tools can build or break down bridges. Most importantly, don't forget to set your own limits.

Practicing a grounding exercise when you feel self-awareness makes an excellent foundation for all exploration throughout the book.

For a detailed list of exercises, refer to chapter 3, section 5.

Chapter 3 - How the Dynamics Play Out in a Board Above and Below the Surface

<u>Why</u>

The most important question you can ask yourself when you enter a board is, "How can I make sure I am heard and understood?" Achieving this is essential to fulfilling your role and taking on your responsibilities on the board. In case you encounter resistance, being aware of your below-the-surface role and the boundaries can help you navigate the unconscious dynamics of the group and still get your message delivered. By voicing these invisible interactions, the group also becomes aware, enabling the whole board to address the impact of psychodynamics on the goal-rational field.

But discussions such as these take time, and boards are always short on it. To carve out a space to discuss psychodynamics, the board must designate time in each meeting and have more meetings throughout the year. Also, ask yourself how many organizations you can meaningfully contribute to if you accord more time to psychodynamics. Don't forget that when you start examining the unconscious zone, the role of diversity should also be considered.

For examples and questions to ask yourself to help address the below-the-surface dynamics, go to Chapter 3, section 2.

What

What Can Go Wrong

Things can go wrong when you do not address psychodynamics at all. On the other hand, being too aware of it can also cause problems. You can use the psychodynamic organizational system framework to structure your exploration of the dynamics of your organization.

Go to Chapter 2, section 3 for examples of what can go wrong and section 4 of the same chapter to refresh your memory about the framework.

What You Need to Know

It is important to understand the difference between a board and the operational organization it oversees. First of all, the board has a double goal which can come into conflict with itself. The board must secure the Return on Equity for the investors while ensuring a running business. These are the two prongs of the primary task. Secondly, the board must set the strategy, handle the finances and make sure that the business complies with regulations, which can also come at odds with each other. This is different from the operational organization that must execute what the board decides on these matters. Finally, the board is a semi-temporary organization, as opposed to the company, which is a permanent one that functions every day of the year. As a board member, you have overall responsibility and accountability for the business which means that you act differently than an employee of the operational organization. Every time you enter the boardroom, you must reevaluate your role to balance the paradoxes inherent in board work.

Staying focused on the primary task, as determined by law, is not always easy. It may be challenged or even redefined. The primary task is also huge and is often split into sub-tasks handled by committees. The chairperson must make sure everyone stays on task, or the work of the whole organization could grind to a halt. This likely means that the board has been distracted from its primary task. A psychodynamic analysis of the situation can help you identify the underlying reasons – maybe the task is scary or there is a power imbalance on the board. In a crisis situation, board members could revert to emergency mode and display fight or flight behaviors, wait for the chairperson to do something or stay silent while two members dominate the conversation. Any of these forces could pull the board off track. But remember, there should always be a balance between taking action and practicing inclusion. If one is neglected for too long, this could also stop progress.

We already learned about the two systems of any organization. These are called the goal-rational field and the psychodynamic field. In the goal-rational field, usually, everyone consciously works on the primary task according to their job definition. This ensures that work progresses – the board is in work-group position. Everyone must also feel that their work has a purpose. Otherwise, they could fall into a basic assumption group in which no work on the primary task is actually happening. A crisis situation could cause this.

In the psychodynamic field, relationships come into play, both on the individual and group level. You may also notice preconscious processes (just below the surface) and unconscious processes (deeply below the surface). Paying attention to your own feelings can give you clues as to what is going on in the invisible zone. When there is uncertainty about boundaries or goals, it could result in regression pressure, which is when one area affects the other. For example, a tragic event in the personal life of a board member could impact the board's ability to work on the primary task. Your board may not be used to discussing these things, but sometimes just making people aware of them can resolve whatever blockage it is causing.

For plenty of examples and a deeper explanation of these concepts, go to Chapter 3, section 4.

What You Need to Do

There are a lot of things you can do to gain awareness of the goal-rational field and the psychodynamic field when you become a member of a board. To familiarize yourself with this field, research the business and all the members of the board. Also, obtain all of the board's available documents. Ask to meet with the chairperson, if possible. Finally, write down what you think the board's primary task is, what its boundaries are and what the role of each member is.

With this information, you can look at the psychodynamic field. Consider the relationships between the board and the operational organization, the board and the owners and between the board members themselves. Write down your thoughts, feelings and fantasies about the tasks, boundaries and roles on the board.

You can then draw up your view of the organization, attend your first board meeting and then revise your view according to what you learned from the encounter. Make sure to pay attention to any warning signs from your analysis. And remember, the analysis never ends.

For more detailed tasks, go to Chapter 3, section 5.

194

Chapter 4 - Personal Emotional Dynamics Worth Understanding

Why

To really understand below-the-surface dynamics and what people are doing unconsciously, you have to learn about a few psychological concepts. First of all, you need to recognize unconscious processes and their effect on the board: the invisible motives and emotions that drive people's behavior. Secondly, be aware of how past relationships and organizational culture influence actions. Thirdly, defense mechanisms that people or groups use to protect themselves can hinder the board's progress. Finally, noticing recurring patterns in relationships, such as recreating a family structure, can give insight as to why people interact the way they do. Pointing out these things can resolve conflicts and misunderstandings.

For examples, go to Chapter 4, section 1.

What

What Can Go Wrong

While taking a psychodynamic perspective can give you insight into how the board functions, remember that all these concepts derive from clinical research. The research, however, can promote development in other fields of society. Also, being overly focused on the dynamics may make you miss other hindrances to progress present in the actual structure of the board.

The above is treated in more detail in Chapter 4, section 2.

What You Need to Know

In the psychodynamic field, some basic mechanisms apply to human behavior in the boardroom and beyond. Understanding these behaviors can help you understand the state of the boardroom and get things moving when progress stalls. These mechanisms are anxiety, projection, transference and countertransference .

Anxiety is a general sense of worry caused by unresolved issues and has the potential to interrupt progress on the task at hand. You can recognize it by noticing your body's signals or if you get distracted. You may also be picking up the anxiety of the group as a whole.

Projection is a defense mechanism. It is when someone is unable to consciously deal with their own uncomfortable emotions and gives it to someone else to express for them. Since the board's time together is short, it is hard to spot the feelings that members bring with them from the outside. But if you are aware of projection, you can determine which feelings are not yours, and which ones are yours and be accountable for them. Projective identification is when the receiver of a projection lives out the feelings of the transmitting person.

Transference is how you map feelings and attitudes from past relationships onto present ones. If you are not aware of it, you may recreate relationship patterns that do not serve you and could rob you of the influence you should have on the board. The relationships and power dynamics on the board may provide a good breeding ground for transference. Be aware that most of the time for most people, transference can be a great help as it allows them to use earlier relational experiences in new relations and situations.

Countertransference, as its name suggests, is a reaction to transference. When someone brings the dynamics of past relationships with them, someone else could fulfill their expectations. The person who may assume that role is engaging in countertransference. It is important to reflect on your relationships on the board and realize what your true feelings are and when you participate in transference and countertransference.

While projection, transference and countertransference are related, it is important to distinguish between them. Projection is when you externalize your emotions in the current moment. Transference is when you bring your internal system, which you learned in the past, into the boardroom, creating a feeling of familiarity. Countertransference is when you engage with others' transference in the recreation of their past relationships.

More detailed definitions of the terminology and many examples can be found in Chapter 4, section 3.

What You Need to Do

To familiarize yourself with the psychological mechanisms, try some of the following suggestions. For anxiety, be mindful of your own triggers and those of others. To identify projection, do the profiling exercise in Chapter 6. Then check in with yourself to uncover overwhelming feelings that are not your own and are not freely expressed in the boardroom. You can discover transference and countertransference by analyzing your family structure. See if you notice any patterns in your professional life or shifts of power on the board. Pay attention to any feelings you have difficulty talking about. Make sure you pinpoint the difference between projection, transference and countertransference by sorting the feelings that are a replay of past patterns from those that are related to the here and now.

These exercises are fleshed out in Chapter 4, section 4.

Chapter 5 - Core Group Dynamics Worth Understanding

Why

Taking a good look at group dynamics will help you understand how regression pressure occurs between the goal-rational field and the psychodynamic field. Having a grasp of the core elements of group dynamics influences decision-making and makes the board more effective. When you recognize the role of unconscious motives and emotions, you can see their influence on board dynamics. Likewise, group dynamics can affect interpersonal relationships, which is particularly pertinent when engaging with diverse perspectives on the board. Managing the dynamics encourages collaboration, governance and open communication, which are all necessary for the board to progress. Analyzing group dynamics together with personal emotional dynamics helps you understand the behavior of each board member.

You can find more details in Chapter 5, section 1.

What

What Can Go Wrong

There can be conflict and miscommunication in the boardroom if you do not manage psychodynamic elements. For example, ignoring unconscious biases could cause ineffective decisions to be made. If roles and relations are not clear, there could be power struggles and a lack of accountability. Without loyalty and trust, there could be governance issues.

You can learn more in Chapter 5, section 2.

What You Need to Know

There are many situations where core group dynamics play out in the boardroom. Some of these are projective room, basic assumption groups, biases – diversity, relations and roles, loyalty to different organizations and finally, trust in the boardroom.

You may have heard the expression FOMO, or the "Fear Of Missing Out." This describes the feeling behind the concept of a projective room, which can be physical or psychological. Whenever a door is closed to you, you wonder what is going on behind it. Likewise, others imagine what is going on in closed rooms that you are in, such as in other boards you are a member of. Projective rooms can serve a purpose, too. For example, the "board's own time" is a closed door to the C-level, but necessary for the board to be able to self-reflect. It is important to be aware of fantasies about projective rooms and communicate clearly about them to relieve any anxiety people may have about them.

For the board to work effectively, it must have a common sense of purpose. Otherwise, it may become a basic assumption group. A basic assumption group is an unconscious state that affects how the group functions and manifests in several ways. The group could operate in a dependent state where they lack agency and rely on the leader. Or they could be in a pairing state in which a non-useful topic is discussed by a few members while the others wait "to be saved." Finally, the group could be in a fight-flight state. In this state, the group avoids the uncertainty around their purpose by creating a conflict (fight) or by discussing a different topic (flight). Keep in mind that the group can shift from one state to another over time, as the focus changes.

Biases are a useful survival technique that allows us to access information rapidly. But they can also prevent you from seeing other points of view or even have you hearing something different than what someone really says because you expect a particular input from them. Being aware of your biases is essential to taking advantage of the diversity on today's boards. There are many different kinds of biases. An anchoring bias is when you only believe the first information you receive. This bias can hinder innovation. Apophenia is another bias in which you seek meaning or patterns where there aren't any. It could cause you to fall prey to the gambler's fallacy. Confirmation bias is when you only ascribe to your own beliefs which can cause tunnel vision.

Hindsight bias makes you believe you already knew the outcome and gives you a false sense of confidence. An availability heuristic bias gives you a preference for future outcomes that you have already experienced. The sunk-cost fallacy is when you continue along a path because you believe that your past investment will eventually bear fruit, even if evidence suggests otherwise. Gender bias relates not only to gender but also to our experiences, culture and personal beliefs. This bias causes you to expect certain behaviors based on stereotypes that prevent you from listening with an open mind.

Being aware of your biases and challenging them makes the board an inclusive and value-generating place. You should also pay attention to people's biases towards you so that you can stand your ground. Remember, it is difficult to change others. But you can change yourself and your own behavior. Having this consciousness and acting on it can make you a more competent board member.

Another thing to be aware of is the relationship between the primary task and your role. Make sure that you are on the board to create value and that you have mutually shared values. What is equally important is to understand the unofficial roles of members of the board. The family structure each member grew up with is a significant factor in board dynamics. The chairperson needs to be acutely aware of this to be able to effectively manage envy and fear of envy when some members are given special tasks, such as committee work. This is especially true during a crisis.

Loyalty to an organization means that you share its values and work towards its goals. From the goal-rational field viewpoint, conflicts of loyalty are always a risk for board members since they are often on more than one board. Before entering a board, make sure to ask yourself if you have any conflicts of interest and voice them. It is also a good idea to disclose any relevant information as this shows that your motives for joining the board are genuine. Remember, when you join a board, it is not to represent an external group. It is to make decisions in the best interest of the company and the stakeholders.

However, conflicts of loyalty can also exist in the psychodynamic field. When you serve on more than one board, you have to decide which one to spend your time on at any given moment. While the best way to handle it is to plan ahead, you may find yourself prioritizing one over the other based on emotional attachment stemming from shared values and personal connections. You may, therefore, be more committed and show more dedication to that organization than others.

Trust between board members, the stakeholders and the operational organization is essential, but there is a built-in paradox. To gain trust, you must first give it. And that means being vulnerable. The chairperson must build a safe boardroom. Likewise, board members must build solid relationships between themselves and the chairperson as well. A psychologically safe boardroom is a place where members are not afraid to speak their minds, share their thoughts, make mistakes and respectfully resolve conflicts. A safe boardroom must also contain safe board members who take responsibility for their roles and are considerate, productive and professional. Achieving and maintaining a safe board requires constant self-exploration. You have to balance being vulnerable against being critical of the behaviors of other board members. The best way to handle this dilemma is to speak up about difficulties with authenticity.

More detailed descriptions of the above situations can be found in Chapter 5, section 3.

What You Need to Do

The above elements appear in many situations. One such situation is the projective room. If you notice yourself imagining what happens in a group you are not a part of, ask questions about it and share about your own groups. The board can shift from working on the primary task to getting stuck in the state of a basic assumption group. You can pick up if your board has fallen into this state by noticing if you are bored, if two people dominate the discussion, if the chairperson seems idolized or if there is heavy arguing while others stay silent. In any of those situations, voice the loss of focus on the primary task.

To spot your biases, reflect on your own assumptions and beliefs and challenge them. Continually listen and educate yourself about other points of view and seek out feedback from those you may be biased toward. Notice the biases of others. If your own biases are a problem, voice them out. To understand your relationship to your role on the board, explore your family structure and notice if you emulate it. Are any family structures being recreated on the board and are they hindering progress? If the board is mature enough, voice your observations and ask for feedback.

To avoid loyalty conflicts, divulge any relevant information to the board when you enter it. Find your own techniques for shifting your mindset when you attend a board meeting, such as saying goodbye to others when you leave your previous environment, changing your clothes, emptying your mind before going into the boardroom and greeting each member of the board. After the meeting, you can note down what emotions you brought with you and what psychological material you absorbed during it.

To verify that *trust* is established on your board, reflect on the following behaviors of the members: if they act consistently or gossip, if people feel comfortable speaking up and if everyone is treated equally. Notice how others respond to you when you speak and also be on the lookout for narcissism or psychopathy. Not all of the above situations will apply to your board, so choose the ones that are useful for you.

These exercises are expanded upon in Chapter 5, section 4.

Chapter 6 - Talent-Based Board Work

Why

In today's complex world, the board needs to be as diverse on the inside as the external environment it is handling on the outside. The success of the organization depends on you bringing different points of view, skills and talents to the table. By also keeping in mind your weaknesses and your capacity to bring out the strengths in others, you can show up with the best possible version of yourself in the boardroom. The possible friction that could arise in a diverse environment is actually a good thing because it breeds new ideas. You are on the board, not only for your competencies, knowledge and skills (which you learned), but most importantly for your inherent talents which are your natural way of seeing, sensing, thinking about and acting in the world. It is your job to develop them and manage them in the boardroom.

For examples of why it is important to understand talents, go to Chapter 6, section 2.

What

What Can Go Wrong

Having diverse minds on the board is key to staying relevant, but you cannot benefit from it unless everyone feels free to speak and express their talents. While your talents may be your biggest asset, they can also be your greatest hindrance if they are too dominant and cause you to be biased. Especially when the pressure is on. When you find another board member annoying, that may actually be their talent coming out. And remember, disagreements can foster new ideas, if well managed.

To learn more about what can go wrong when you apply your talents, go to Chapter 6, section 3.

What You Need to Know

Modern boards need to be able to adapt to all the external pressures being placed on them. When strategizing, you need to know how to leverage your talents appropriately so you can bring value to the board. Your board is faced with complicated situations for which you can predict the outcome. However, when things get complex, you don't know how they will turn out. Be aware of the difference so you know which talent to apply and when. It also exposes your own biases, which helps you make the choice.

To be able to handle complexity, emergent strategizing is a useful tool. While classic strategizing assumes predictability – in other words, that the decision-makers are rational and they already know all the causes – this may not be valid in the current business market. Emergent strategizing is based on cultural observations of what actually happens in strategy work because, in reality, developing a strategy is neither linear nor are the decision makers necessarily rational. It is your job to apply both classical and emergent techniques and use your talents accordingly.

In the past, boards set a five-year plan. While it is still useful to plan ahead, building an emergent strategy is a constant balance between observing, testing and adjusting. To use the emergent method, you can look at the 3Ps: What are the group's Practices? What are the roles of the Practitioners? And what is their Praxis – that is, what do they actually do during strategizing? The 3Ps help you think critically about the board's collaboration and lead to better decisions.

New strategizing techniques are not enough. The board needs cognitive diversity, or put more simply, many different perspectives. Therefore, you must bring all your unique talents to the boardroom and be aware of your biases. But to be able to apply your talents effectively, they have to "fit." First of all, you have to determine which of your personal talents fit the task at hand. Or maybe none of them do, as you cannot always be the best person for the job. This is a person-task fit. Another kind of fit is person-group fit. When your talents overlap with others in the group, this is a complimentary group fit. When your talents fill in the gaps, this is a supplementary group fit. Both kinds are useful.

Achieving a fit takes effort. First, the group's values and goals must be clearly stated and everyone needs to demonstrate how their talents can contribute. Secondly, each board member needs to look at how they fit with other board members, the executive team and the stakeholders. Your interactions with each of these groups bring out certain talents. It's important to pay attention to this as it encourages diversity and ultimately, good decision-making. In addition to strategy, the primary task of the board is to protect shareholder interests by ensuring a running business that is compliant with proper governance and risk management and to hire (or at least approve) members of the C-suite. Your unique combination of talents will probably match up differently to these tasks of board work.

For deeper definitions and more detailed examples, go to Chapter 6, section 4.

What You Need to Do

The first thing you need to do is discover your profile by taking a specialized talent test. Talent tests give you a vocabulary to use when talking about your strengths and weaknesses. They also show the full range of your potential, as well as the drawbacks. With this inventory, you can plan how to develop and control your talents.

Your talents are like an incomplete toolbox. To best benefit from your tools, you have to practice using them and collaborate with others to complete your box. We all have a tendency to reach for our favorite tool in every situation, but personal talent development is about learning how to apply the right tool at the right time. However, unlike a real toolbox, you can not add to it. It is important to admit that you are incomplete. Ideally, someone on the board has what you are missing.

For details on the different talent tests, examples and scenarios, refer to Chapter 6, section 5.

Chapter 7 - How to Understand Dynamics in the Board Committees

Why

With more topics than ever to deal with, boards need committees to be able to address them all. But all these committees change the dynamics of the board and open new opportunities to cross boundaries. A committee can create a great deal of value for the board by reducing the workload and leveraging the specialized skills of certain board members. To do so, they must be accountable and communicate effectively so that the board can make informed decisions. Committees preprocess the information for the board as well as access new perspectives when they cross boundaries into the operational organization or customer groups. These situations create a space for learning.

However, when you add committees into the mix, board members become required to meet more often and under different circumstances. In addition, their interactions across boundaries also contribute to a change in board dynamics. It affects the goal-rational field by giving some board members more knowledge about the operational organization. The psychodynamic field is also impacted because new relationships and unconscious groups form. Sometimes hidden subgroups emerge, both based on tasks, talents or shared interests and identifications. Roles and priorities on the board may also end up changing.

Committees can be a space for learning, but they cannot create a pure learning community since they must ultimately bring value to the board. However, applying a light version of a learning space to a committee can be beneficial not only to itself but can even be eventually expanded to the board.

What

What Can Go Wrong

While creating more committees can optimize board work, it also requires more management and communication. These two areas are prone to break down. A committee must have clear points of reference, expectations and a common understanding to be able to progress. Alternatively, a committee can become so knowledgeable that they end up making decisions on their specific topic, rather than leaving it to the board. Committees have more interaction with the operational organization, so there is a risk of becoming too involved. As an individual, when you show up to a committee meeting with your talents, you may come on too strongly which can cause tension if not well managed.

Creating a learning space in a committee also comes with risks. A conflict between the need to produce something for the board at a certain time and the need to learn freely so that they can produce something valuable may arise.

What You Need to Know

Everything this book has taught you up until this point can be applied to committees. You need to be conscious, use the psychodynamic organizational systems framework and the talents framework, as well as implement a learning space.

First, it is important to know the difference between a "pure" learning space and the adapted form that can be used in a committee. A "pure" learning space has the sole purpose of promoting learning, with a facilitator who guides and encourages collaboration. A committee that incorporates learning shares these elements, but is more structured and must eventually produce a product for the board.

In your committee, you can promote learning by encouraging open conversations among members at meetings or workshops. To create good communication, empathy and teamwork, everyone on the committee should be conscious of self-awareness, self-management, social awareness, relationship skills and social responsibility. As part of good communication, the committee needs to develop a common language that fosters mutual understanding and a safe space. When committees do self-assessments of their effectiveness, they should also look at how effective their learning is, find areas of improvement and make sure they stay aligned with the charter of the board.

As with all learning spaces, a committee should have a facilitator, often the committee chair. This person creates a safe space by making sure everyone has the opportunity to contribute, building trust, encouraging independence among members and cultivating social relationships. The chairperson can use different group methods such as voicing group dynamics or physically creating a learning space, such as sitting in a circle.

As a member of a committee, you should be keenly aware of your own agency and that of the other members. Ask questions out of curiosity and see if others are willing to put themselves in the same insecure position. When you are willing to take the first step, you support a learning environment. By communicating respectfully, sharing knowledge, and practicing empathy and active listening, you also encourage learning and building relationships. In this way, you can implement a learning environment within the structure of a committee. Remember that committee work is done on the boundary between the board, the operational organization and, possibly, the customers. While this is challenging, a successful learning space can indeed be created.

See Chapter 7, section 4 for a more detailed description and practical use cases of dynamics in a committee and of the light learning model in a committee.

What You Need to Do

You can enhance value creation in your committees by understanding committee work through the lens of the psychodynamic organizational system view, psychological mechanisms and talent appreciation. The following exercises also help you develop and support a learning environment in your committee.

To understand committees above the surface, be familiar with the committee charter, the particular subject it will be addressing and the official roles of the members. Below the surface, analyze the dynamics, both of the group and your own internal system. If there are any issues, voice and address them.

To apply talents to committees, identify the talents needed then find the people who possess them. Name the talents on the board and point out any missing ones. Identify your own talents and decide which to turn up and which to turn down as a function of the committee's needs.

To develop and support a learning space in your committee, give and show trust, be self-aware, curious, inclusive, and vulnerable and support others who do the same.

For more detailed exercises that you can do to enhance your committee work, go to Chapter 7, section 5.

Conclusion and Onwards

Let us refer back to the questions in the introduction of this book. Do you now have an idea of how to change your trajectory away from not being fully present, not really meeting your goals nor truly working as a group? I would hope so!

This book's journey has come to an end. You have watched a bridge being built between organizational understanding and the board environment. You now understand and know how to work with dynamics on the board, both as an individual member and with your fellow board members. As you go into your next board meeting, you will have a new point of view. You can now show up with more confidence and competence in your role as a chairperson or member, whether on the board or in the committees.

You have learned how to apply your own agency and consciousness to what goes on both above and below the surface. You are aware of which talents to tap into and when. Therefore, you are better equipped to be a value-creating board member. You have the necessary foundation to make a difference on both the board and in the committees. You can enhance how a board works together in an environment that is safe and encourages learning.

This is of significant importance to modern boards since they are navigating a highly vibrant geopolitical era. The board is overloaded with new topics and must follow technological developments such as AI and cybersecurity, compliance requirements and climate change. Moreover, good governance is gaining priority on the agenda as a result of expectations from stakeholders and increased scrutiny of the practices of organizations. Recognition of good governance, such as diversity, leads to better organizational performance so it is not surprising that it is high up on the board's agenda.

Boards vary from country to country. Even within a single country, there are different cultures. How the dynamics play out depends on which developmental state the organization is in, the ownership, the number of members on the board, the type of members, regulations, the financial situation, strategic partnerships, the industry and the operational organization – just to name a few.

However, looking at the board through the lens of organizational understanding, you will notice that this lens is universal. The board is a group of people working together who have a common task – split in two – to carry out. The board must ensure that the owners profit from their investment, be it monetary, intangible or any equivalent measure of success. The board sets the strategy and oversees that the operational organization implements it to run a sound and compliant business.

Below the surface, the board works like any regular group of people. This is where the universal nature of organizational dynamics comes in. You, as a person, affect the group and the group affects you. What you bring with you from other places impacts the board meeting. How you expect the organization to run influences the board meeting. Whether these elements are preconscious, conscious or unconscious will make a difference in how the dynamics play out in the room. Those that you are aware of, you can work with.

So, consciousness is key to working with dynamics. It is your most valuable tool for ensuring that the board proceeds with the work at hand and does not get into confusing conflicts. It can prevent the board from morphing from a working group into the state of a basic assumption group that does not work on the primary task.

Being conscious of the talents required in different areas of the board is essential to being efficient. It is indispensable for individuals who want to turn up and turn down their talents accordingly.

Awareness of boundaries is crucial for respecting and fulfilling your role as a board member, not only in the board meetings but especially as a committee member. The committee stands on the boundary between the board and the organization. Working at that frontier creates a space for learning as well as for conflicts. Navigating this gray area is a challenge for the board chairpersons, the members and the organization.

Building the bridge between a goal-rational orientation and psychological understanding is your toolbox to becoming more conscious of yourself and the dynamics of today's active and diverse boards.

This book, as well as the organization created to run this book, is coming to an end. The outcome of the process has been a product delivered by an operational organization with a diverse board, writers and myself, who carried out multiple roles. We have been through everything a startup usually experiences. We have been frustrated and asked ourselves questions like where the product is and what our board's purpose is. We have also brought on new board members and new writers and figured out how to finance the business.

I am grateful for this journey and I hope you have enjoyed your own journey reading this book. Building bridges is what we need in today's world so that we can listen, learn and make proper decisions for our businesses.

To excel with your new toolbox, you can practice further by going through the cases described in the bonus material. It can be found at www.kromanns.com/boarddynamics.

The bonus material also includes what did not make it into the book but is definitely worth digging into. You can find references in case you would like to dive deeper into the areas presented here. Moreover, you will find dedicated material for the role of the chairperson.

To support your own continuous journey I encourage you to listen to the podcasts with various board members, experienced and new, as well as people from various places in the world with diverse knowledge and backgrounds. Please search for "Board Dynamics - An international view" or head to www.kromanns.com/boarddynamics.

Finally, I suggest that you look up worldwide organizations around the world where you can join training groups in psychodynamic understanding, take a talent test or find communities of practice. Some useful links may be found at www.kromanns.com/boarddynamics.

Boards have one focus: to develop a successful and compliant business. To be efficient, you as a board member should recognize and manage unconscious biases and interpersonal dynamics that may otherwise hinder decision-making and collaboration. To be a high-performing board, all members should do the same.

This is the bridge-building suggested by this book.

A big thank you to everybody who has contributed to making both the book and the podcast series blossom.

Appendix A: The Organization Behind This Book

The word organization can be used in many different contexts. In this appendix, I use the word to refer to the formal organizational structure of this book, run as a company. I chose to set up a professional board to live the word of the book and to explore the dynamics as they played out on our board.

The Board Dynamics organization was established in 2022 with the purpose of spreading knowledge on how dynamics can play out in a Board of Directors, whether in the boardroom, in the committees or in between the formal meetings.

The outcome, or you could say product, produced by this organization is a published practical book that helps new board members enter and work on the board, with a focus on what is happening underneath the surface.

There are many programs that will teach you all about the tangible areas and responsibilities of fulfilling your role as a board member. But by understanding the dynamics under the surface – the intangible aspects – you will learn how to show up as both competent and confident in your new role.

The organization "Board Dynamics" lives what it preaches. This is done by establishing a dedicated board of directors to lead this book's production.

The board of directors was set up to be as diverse as possible, with both the original group and additional members elected based on this principle The multi-role dynamic was also played out since the owner, the chair and the CEO are one person. We acted like a start-up eager to run 90 miles an hour, which added healthy tension when faced with our need to comply with the "Rules of Procedures" and good governance.

We had our ups and downs throughout the production of this book, something we became acutely aware of thanks to the way we frame our board meetings. We made sure to lean into and understand what was going on under the surface. Before meetings, each individual spent five minutes after arrival to prepare a pre-brief, and after, we debriefed by sharing with other members our thoughts and feelings on how the meeting turned out.

This gave us data to study the dynamics in the board of directors – a temporary organization that started with an idea and ended with the publication of this book. In addition, the board of directors worked differently from an operational organization since we only acted as a group four to six times a year.

In our board, you will find members with varied skills and experiences to support the subject, a board of directors focused on diversity in all respects.

The Idea

Below is the idea that started the creation of this book.

The development of boards:

- 10 years back: Boards started the journey of good governance – "old boys' network"

- Right now: Active and value-creating diverse boards

- Next 10 years: Active boards work as an organization where the psychology in the organization is key to fulfilling the purpose of the board – "value-creating and diverse board"

Challenges:

- Active boards require active leadership

- Organizational management requires an understanding of psychology in the organization above and below the surface

- More active boards mean a broader and partial interface with the organization, and as such broader and individual transference between the board and organization

- Diversity requires an understanding of the full person

Solution:

- Handbook with cases to understand psychology in the board and get concrete actions for board members, the chairperson and other roles

The Annual Wheel

Below is the annual wheel of the Board Dynamics' Board of Directors.

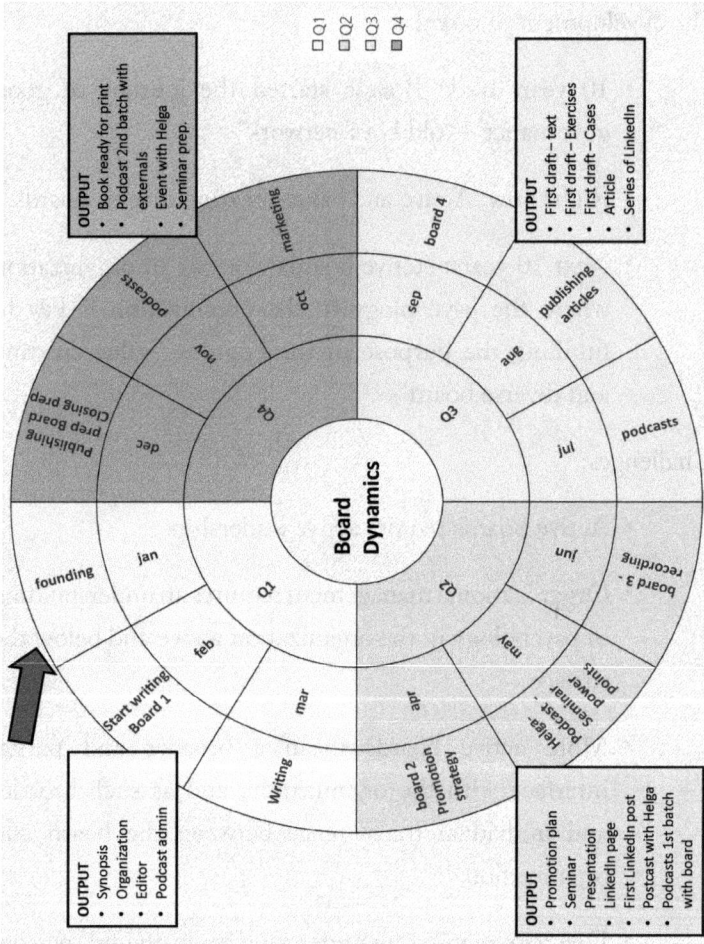

Annual wheel

4/1/2025

Board Members

Annette Lang Skovbølling – ASEO Invest: Investor, CEO, Board Professional, Denmark

Ashley Morris – Progressive Media, Podcast Mentor, UK

Dorrit Kromann – Kromanns, Board Professional, Board Dynamics Handbook Founder, Author, Denmark

Leo Smith – Partner in Talents Unlimited, PhD on Organizational Mentoring as Strategic HR Practice

Lesley Antoun – Lesley Antoun Consulting, President, Board Professional, Canada

Paul Diponkar – OMERS, Associate Director, Data Platform Engineering, Canada

Peter Koefoed – Peter Koefoed, Cand.Psych.Aut. Specialist and Supervisor in Psychotherapy and Organizational Psychology, Denmark

Phaedria Marie St. Hilaire – Phaedria Marie Consulting, CEO and Chief Consultant, Board Professional, Denmark

Authors

Dorrit Kromann – Kromanns, Board Professional, Board Dynamics Handbook Founder, Author, Denmark

Leo Smith – Partner in Talents Unlimited, PhD on Organizational Mentoring as Strategic HR Practice

Publisher

Inspired By Publishing, as led by Chloë Bisson

Editor

Deborah Schindelman

Podcast Editor

"Progressive Media" – Ashley Morris

Graphics

"Aftryk" – Sabitha Jørgensen

Appendix B: Introducing the Board Dynamics Board Members

Let me introduce myself first. It is I, **Dorrit Kromann,** who was behind the idea of the book. I have worked in the cross-section between business leadership and organizational psychology my entire work life. I'm Danish, live in Denmark and have always been passionate about learning and understanding. I am an experienced board professional and investor.

Annette Lang Skovbølling. Annette is also Danish and lives in Denmark. Annette is a serial entrepreneur and investor, so she has seen many of the dynamics that evolve as a company goes from start-up to scale-up to fully fledged corporation. I met Annette through a recommendation from my network.

Ashley Morris. Ashley is based in the UK and comes with a very different set of competencies. Ashley is a podcast consultant and expert client manager at a digital media company. Ashley brings very fresh perspectives to our discussions and meetings. I got to know Ashley through networking after I had posted to LinkedIn a link by Andrea Petrone on diversity. We connected and he recommended Ashley to produce my podcasts. I asked Ashley if he would be "the young and new in boards" member and here we are now.

Leo Smith. Leo has a PhD in Organizational Mentoring and lives in Denmark. Leo brings a wealth of knowledge on organizations and talents in boards, such as what is needed in which type of board. One chapter of the book is about knowing how to use your own personal talents and Leo signed up to write it. I know Leo from a recommendation in a seminar on angel investments provided by Nykredit Wealth and DANBAN.

Lesley Antoun. Lesley is Canadian and is an experienced executive with extensive board experience. Through direct board memberships as well as advisory roles, Lesley has extensive knowledge of the dynamics in boards. I met Lesley through a recommendation from Andrea Petrone. I have a lot to be thankful to Andrea for.

Paul Diponkar. Paul lives in Toronto, Canada. He has held various tech leadership roles and has a deep understanding of how technology impacts processes and organizations. He leads one of the largest Data Professionals Communities (non-profit) in Canada. With a diverse background, Diponkar grew up in South Asia, attended universities in Sweden and the UK, and spent over a decade building his career and family in Denmark. I got to know him and his lovely family when we, as part of a larger group, organized a charity concert for Bangladesh.

Peter Koefoed. Peter is a Cand.psych.aut (Master of Psychology), group analyst, specialist and supervisor in psychotherapy, occupational and organizational psychology. Peter is our heavy hitter when it comes to psychology. He helps us to look at our hypothesis through an academic and practical lens. Peter is also Danish and lives in Denmark. I met Peter when I took my Masters in Organizational Psychology. He was part of the team that developed this new education back in 2001, the first time psychodynamic organizational theory was considered formal education and worthy of stand-alone education in Denmark.

This was the time when dynamics in operational organizations became part of the organizational understanding.

Phaedria Marie St. Hilaire. Phaedria has many years of executive experience in Life Science and also works as a business angel and board professional. She now lives in Denmark but was born in Dominica and educated in the US. She therefore has some insight into minorities and is an active and strong player at this stage. I got to know Phaedria at one of the events where she showed up to talk about female investors at Angela Invest. I reached out and she found the book and organization interesting to support.

I'm truly grateful to these seven fantastic people who chose to join me on this journey.

Thank you!

References

Introduction

1. Gevurtz, F.A., 'The historical and political origins of the corporate board of directors', Hofstra Law Review: Vol. 33: Iss. 1, Article 3, 2004, p.16

2. Vilsbæk, L., "Men hvor finder man bestyrelsesposterne?", nyibestyrelsen, 1 August 2019, https://www.nyibestyrelsen.dk/blogposts/hvor-finder-jeg-en-bestyrelsespost (access date: 24 November 2024).

3. Bruchmann, J. & Vingtoft, O., "Who are we?", nboard, https://nboard.dk/about, (access date: 24 November 2024).

4. Dame Vivian Hunt et al., 'Diversity matters even more: The case for holistic impact', McKinsey, 2023, https://www.mckinsey.com/featured-insights/diversity-and-inclusion/diversity-matters-even-more-the-case-for-holistic-impact (access date: 24 November 2024).

5. Podcast with Charles Stonehill 6 September 2024 www.kromanns.com/boarddynamics

Chapter 1

6. Carpintero, H., 'History of Organizational Psychology', Oxford Research Encyclopedia of Psychology, 2017, https://oxfordre.com/psychology/display/10.1093/acrefore/9780190236557.001.0001/acrefore-9780190236557-e-39 (access date: 24 November 2024);

    Powers, K., Workplace psychology: Issues and Application, Pressbooks.pub, 2019, https://pressbooks.pub/workplacepsychology/, (access date: 24 November 2024).

7. Bonnerup, B., Et psykodynamisk blik på levende organisationer, Akademisk Forlag, 2024, p.28.

8. Bonnerup, B. Et psykodynamisk blik på levende organisationer. Akademisk Forlag, 2024, p. 25.

9. Ten Governing Documents Every Board Member Needs, BoardSpot, https://www.boardspot.com/ten-governing-documents-every-board-member-needs, (access date: 24. November 2024).

10. Visholm, S., "Organisationspsykologi og psykodynamisk systemteori". in T Heinskou & S Visholm (ed.), Psykodynamisk organisationspsykologi: På arbejde under overfladen. Hans Reitzels Forlag, Copenhagen, 2004.

Chapter 2

11. Heller, L., & Kammer, B. J. (2022). The practical guide for healing developmental trauma: using the neuroaffective relational model to address adverse childhood experiences and resolve complex trauma. North Atlantic Books. p. 9.

12. Encyclopædia Britannica, Boundary, 2024, The Britannica Dictionary, https://www.britannica.com/dictionary/boundary, (access date: 24 November 2024).

13. Bonnerup, B., Et psykodynamisk blik på levende organisationer, Akademisk Forlag, 2024.

14. Heller, L., & Kammer, B. J. (2022). The practical guide for healing developmental trauma: using the neuroaffective relational model to address adverse childhood experiences and resolve complex trauma. North Atlantic Books. p. 166.

15. Gionta, D. & Guerra,D., From Stressed to Centered: A Practical Guide to a Healthier and Happier You, Santa Barbara, Sea Hill Press Inc., 2015.

Chapter 3

16. M. Matzon, 'Her er det værste, du kan sige på jobbet', Djoefbladet, October 24, 2024., https://www.djoefbladet.dk/artikler/2024/10/det-vaerste-ord-jobbet-afstemning-liste, (access date: 24 November 2024).

17. Bonnerup, B., Et psykodynamisk blik på levende organisationer, Akademisk Forlag, 2024, p. 63;

Visholm, S & Koefoed, "Følelser i organisationer: psykodynamiske perspektiver", in T Heinskou & S Visholm (eds.), Psykodynamisk organisationspsykologi II: På mere arbejde under overfladerne. Hans Reitzels Forlag, Copenhagen, 2011, p.68;

Heinskou T, Visholm S (ed.). Psykodynamisk organisationspsykologi II: På mere arbejde under overfladerne. Hans Reitzels Forlag, 2011, p. 70.

18. Axelbank, J., "Using Future Search to Address Wicked Systemic Problems", NJ Psychologist, vol. 72, no. 3, 2022, p. 10 (Gordian Knot is a metaphor for wicked problems)

19. The Danish Business Authority, 'Board', The Company Guide, https://virksomhedsguiden.dk/content/ydelser/bestyrelse/c6040749-edd2-460a-86cb-4626b3509fb7/, (access date: 24 November 2024).

20. Heinskou, T. & Visholm, S. (eds), Psykodynamisk organisationspsykologi: På arbejde under overfladen. Hans Reitzels Forlag, Copenhagen, 2004., p. 37;

Bonnerup, B., Et psykodynamisk blik på levende organisationer, Akademisk Forlag, 2024, p 31

21. Bonnerup, B., Et psykodynamisk blik på levende organisationer, Akademisk Forlag, 2024, p 35

22. Heinskou, T & Visholm, S (eds), Psykodynamisk organisationspsykologi: På arbejde under overfladen. Hans Reitzels Forlag, Copenhagen, 2004. Chapter: «Arbejdsgruppen og grundantagelsesgruppen»

23. Bonnerup, B., Et psykodynamisk blik på levende organisationer, Akademisk Forlag, 2024, p 27

24. Bonnerup, B., Et psykodynamisk blik på levende organisationer, Akademisk Forlag, 2024, p 99

25. Bonnerup, B., Et psykodynamisk blik på levende organisationer, Akademisk Forlag, 2024, p 40

26. Bonnerup, B., Et psykodynamisk blik på levende organisationer, Akademisk Forlag, 2024, p 43

27. Bonnerup, B., Et psykodynamisk blik på levende organisationer, Akademisk Forlag, 2024, p 46

Chapter 4

28. Bonnerup, B., Et psykodynamisk blik på levende organisationer, Akademisk Forlag, 2024, p. 25

29. Kranz, Koefoed, Visholm: Organisationsforandring og psykodynamisk forståelse 1, Erhvervspsykologi, Vol 2, No 3, Sep. 2004

30. Kets de Vries, M., & Cheak, A. "Psychodynamic Approach". In P. Northouse (Ed.), Leadership: Theory and Practice (7th ed., pp. 363-396). Thousand Oaks, CA: Sage. (2016).

31. Bonnerup, B., Et psykodynamisk blik på levende organisationer, Akademisk Forlag, 2024, p. 40

32. Bonnerup, B., Et psykodynamisk blik på levende organisationer, Akademisk Forlag, 2024, p 85

33. Encyclopædia Britannica, Projection, 2024, The Britannica Dictionary, https://www.britannica.com/science/projection-psychology, (access date: 24 November 2024).

34. Bonnerup, B., Et psykodynamisk blik på levende organisationer, Akademisk Forlag, 2024, p 308, p.139.

35. Moore, B. E., & Fine, B. D. (Eds.). Psychoanalytic terms and concepts. American Psychoanalytic Association; Yale University Press., 1990, p. 196

36. Diamond, M., & Allcorn, S. "The Cornerstone of Psychoanalytic Organizational Analysis: Psychological Reality, Transference and Counter-Transference in the Workplace". Human Relations, 56(4), 2003, pp. 491-514.

37. 'Transference & Counter-Transference', Counselling Tutor, https://counsellingtutor.com/transference-and-countertransference/, (access date: 24 November 2024).

Chapter 5

38. Heinskou, T. & Visholm, S. (eds), Psykodynamisk organisationspsykologi: På arbejde under overfladen. Hans Reitzels Forlag, Copenhagen, 2004.,

39. Heinskou, T., Visholm, S. (ed.). Psykodynamisk organisationspsykologi II: På mere arbejde under overfladerne. Hans Reitzels Forlag, 2011.

40. A. Tobena, I. Marks, R. Dar, "Advantages of bias and prejudice: an exploration of their neurocognitive templates", Neuroscience & Biobehavioral Reviews, Volume 23, Issue 7, 1999, pp. 1047-1058

41. Odih, R. 'The Implications, Challenges, and Solutions of Boardroom Bias', Actuate, August 29, 2024, https://actuateglobal.com/news-resources/the-implications-challenges-and-solutions-of-boardroom-bias/, (access date: 24 November 2024);

Adfærdsdesign," Børsen Uddannelses masterclass, 8th and 9th June 2021, https://borsen.dk/uddannelse/masterclass/adfaerdsdesign/, (access date: 13. January 2025)

42. S. Visholm, "The Promoted Sibling: New perspectives in family and group dynamics", Siblings: Rivalry and envy - coexistence and concern, Krakow, Poland, 2011.

43. Leo, "The Psychology Behind Loyalty: Defining Its True Meaning - Psychology", Psychologily, October 8, 2023, https://psychologily.com/loyalty-definition-psychology/, (access date: 24 November 2024).

44. Peter Koefoed: Kahn, P., "Holding Environments at Work." In The Journal of Applied Behavioral Science, Vol. 37 No. 3, 2001, pp. 260-279.

45. Abrahams, D., & Rohleder, P. (2021). A Clinical Guide to Psychodynamic Psychotherapy (1st ed.). Routledge.

46. Gallo, A. "What is psychological safety", Harvard Business Review, February 15, 2023, https://hbr.org/2023/02/what-is-psychological-safety, (access date: 24 November 2024).

47. "Creating a Psychologically Safe Space for Better Collaboration," Groupmap, https://www.groupmap.com/2022/04/14/creating-a-psychologically-safe-space-for-better-collaboration, (access date: 24 November 2024).

Chapter 6

48. Clifton, D. O. & Harter, J. (2003). Investing in Strengths. In A. K.S. Cameron, B. J.E.

49. Chandler, A.D., Strategy and Structure: Chapters in the History of American Enterprise, Boston, MIT Press, 1962.

50. Mintzberg, H., "Patterns in Strategy Formation," Management Science, vol. 24, no. 9,), May 1978, pp. 934-948

51. Vaara, E. & Whittington, R., "Strategy-as-Practice: Taking Social Practice Seriously," The Academy of Management Annals, 2012, pp. 285-336.

52. Ashby, W. R., An Introduction to Cybernetics, London, Chapman & Hall, 1956.

53. Reynolds, A. Lewis, D., "Teams solve problems faster when they're more cognitively diverse," Harvard Business Review, March 2017.

54. Kristof-Brown, A. L., Schneider, B. & Su, R. (2023). Person-Organisation fit theory and Research: Conondrums, Conclusion, and Calls to Action. Personnel Psychology, 76, 375-412

55. Seong, J. Y., Kristof-Brown, A. L., Park, W., Hong, D., and Shin, Y., "Person-Group Fit: Diversity Antecedents, Proximal, and Performance at the Group Level," Journal of Management, vol. 41, iss. 4, 2015, pp. 1184-1213.

Chapter 7

56. "Creating and Working Well with Diverse Committees", University of Victoria - Equity and Human Rights, https://www.uvic.ca/equity/assets/docs/diversity.pdf), (access date: 24 November 2024).

57. Wiggers, M. Exploring the role of the facilitator in learning communities supporting team learning and reflexivity, MA diss., University of Twente, 2024, p. 9.

58. Huguet, Alice, Heather L. Schwartz, and Catherine H. Augustine, "Building an Effective Social and Emotional Learning Committee in Dallas: One of Six Case Studies of Schools and Out-of-School-Time Program Partners", Volume 2, Part 3. Santa Monica, CA: RAND Corporation, 2022.;

"5 Social Emotional Learning (SEL) Classroom Management Techniques", The Incredible Years, May 22, 2024, https://www.incredibleyears.com/blog/social-emotional-teaching-strategies, (access date: 24 November 2024).

59. "Social learning: History, application, and key factors for success", Rapl, October 6, 2023, https://getrapl.com/blog/social-learning-history-application-and-key-factors-for-success/, (access date: 24 November 2024).

www.ingramcontent.com/pod-product-compliance
Lightning Source LLC
Chambersburg PA
CBHW071158210326
41597CB00016B/1587